THE HIGHER EDUCATION SCENE IN AMERICA

Some Observations

Abraham L. Gitlow and Howard S. Gitlow

D1566955

University Press of America,® Inc.
Lanham · Boulder · New York · Toronto · Plymouth, UK

Copyright © 2014 by
University Press of America,® Inc.
4501 Forbes Boulevard
Suite 200
Lanham, Maryland 20706
UPA Acquisitions Department (301) 459-3366

10 Thornbury Road
Plymouth PL6 7PP
United Kingdom

Library of Congress Control Number: 2014946796
ISBN: 978-0-7618-6458-5 (paperback : alk. paper)
eISBN: 978-0-7618-6459-2

Contents

Preface

America's universities and colleges are at the apex of world-wide respect as institutions of learning—passing on accumulated knowledge, and extending the borders of that knowledge. Above all, they are characterized by their freedom of inquiry and discussion. Unfortunately, that is partly an illusion. All is not perfect within the halls of Academe. There are dangers that threaten the future of these institutions. Some are obvious, like the corrupting influence of Division I sports programs. Others are subtle, like conflicts of interest between faculty responsibility for service within the university and remunerative commitments that are external to the institution and its needs. We attempt, in this small volume, to expose those dangers, and to suggest how they may be overcome. As we begin our inquiry with a look at the mission of higher education in a free society, two questions immediately confront us: (1) What is the mission of for-profit institutions in higher education? (2) What is the mission of on-line learning and MOOCs (Massive, Open, On-line, Courses)?

As the twenty-first century opened, for-profit universities and colleges were burgeoning institutions, enrolling thousands of students, and financed by a flood of federal funds. It seemed that our traditional interactive teacher-student relationship was threatened by an impersonal methodology. Then came MOOCs! The threat became an overnight nightmare; an educational revolution appeared to be underway. But reality reasserted itself. Scandalous recruiting practices by the for-profit institutions became public. A leaner, more responsible for-profit sector remained to serve students unready for the traditional nonprofit curriculum. The for-profit sector of higher education focused primarily on performing the employability mission. MOOCs underwent modifications, and are being digested by the existing nonprofit institutions, albeit at a moderate pace as further modifications make them more digestible.

A more subtle danger lurks beneath the academic surface. It involves the diffusion of power and authority in our higher education institutions as opposed to power emanating from formal status. Unlike commercial corporations, decision making is not centered in a group of administrative executives. Major matters such as curriculum, new faculty hires and replacement, as well as promotion and tenure decisions are reserved to the tenured and tenure-track faculty. The US Supreme Court's Yeshiva University decision of some 40 years ago (which applied to private non-profit institutions), made faculty part of management and, unlike employees, subject to industrial relations rules. A substantive dialogue is required between the institutions' administrators and the faculty. A consensus needs to be arrived at, but it may not be easy. It certainly requires the attention of the faculty, but their time is now too often diverted to remunerative alternatives external to the institution, especially in the research universities sector.

A further source of internal tension and possible strife resides in the pecking order found in the academic community. The PhD is the foundation for academic status. It is a requirement for appointment to a tenure-track professorship. Other doctorates have prestige, but not quite as much (doctorates related to professional areas of study). The subtle differences are a source of internal tension between the faculties of Arts & Sciences and those of the professional schools in the university. In those differences resides room for quarrels over the institution's mission, e.g., the mission to create and disseminate knowledge, and develop critical thinking, versus training students for jobs.

Also a source of mischief, but more serious, is the profound shift in faculty staffing profiles that has occurred over the past half century in our universities and colleges. As remunerative research opportunities mushroomed, the time spent teaching students by full-time tenured and tenure-track faculty shrank, from approximately 70% to some 30%. The empowered faculty in the classroom were replaced by full-time and part-time contingent faculty. They became 70% of the instructional staff, while only 30% continued to be possessors of institutional power. Frustration and resentment rose. Unionization seemed to offer an antidote. That route, however, undermined the academic ideal of shared governance, and promised protest and strife. It also brought the university and college ever closer to the corporate model.

No less serious a danger is the current primacy of financial demands on the attention and time of the leaders (presidents and academic deans) of non-profit higher education institutions. Presumably academic leaders, they now spend almost all their days, and many evenings, dealing with fundraising and budgets. Academic issues are the province of provosts. The number two executive deals with the heart of the institution, while the number one leader wrestles with money. It is a reversal of formal power that does not offer comfort to those who worry about the long-term survival of the independent research university.

The fundraising challenge is especially demanding of the time of presidents, supported by staffs of professional fundraisers. It is significant that graduate degrees are now awarded to trained fundraisers. We discuss multiple sources of funds, and suggest ways to make them productive. Note is made of a simple fact: a prolific fundraising president or dean draws power and administrative authority from that ability, an ability that is derived from knowledge and/or charisma. Endowments receive our attention as an important asset, and a means of easing periods of financial strain. Consideration is given to the demands made by partisans of various socially and politically correct causes to invest endowments as they would prefer, and often boycotting otherwise-sound investments. They ignore the fiduciary responsibility of fund trustees to seek the maximum return for the benefit of the academic mission. Throughout there is the insidious challenge of accepting large donations that have such strings attached as establishing institutes, centers, or endowed professorships that do not a fit with the institution's academic mission, or are not properly funded into the future. Worse, and morally abhorrent, is the gift that seeks some preference for an unsuited student, or "buys" a seat on the board.

Hard on the heels of this litany of dangers to the academic integrity of higher education come two potentially mortal hazards, one lurking beneath the surface (conflicts of interest), the other overt and blatant (Division I sports programs). Conflicts of interest are a malevolent and corrupting influence, centered principally on remunerative connections of faculty and administrators with persons and organizations external to the university. For example, consider a tenured physician in the medical school who has a relationship with a pharmaceutical company concerning a drug she or he has a financial interest in. On the one hand, they draw away from the institution the service and teaching obligations of its academic staff—a grievous loss to shared governance. On the other hand, they can involve seriously damaging financial arrangements between academicians and outside organizations and individuals. To manage them, clear statements of university policy are necessary—statements that define in crystal-clear language what is prohibited and the consequences of infractions.

Division I sports programs are neither a subtle nor harmless source of student and alumni fun. They are blatantly corrupting as the NCAA's flood of money enriches head football and basketball coaches, while promoting the myth of student/athletes and exploiting them. Those programs impact the courses of study, inviting the creation of fictitious courses, fraudulent grade inflation, unearned credits, and possible graduation with an unwarranted diploma. It distorts the compensation structure of the academic entity, inviting intra-institutional inequities and stress. All in all, it is a cancer in the academic body that must be excised. But how can it be done? All that money and the evil it instills is already in the bloodstream of the Academy. Three approaches are discussed—two unlikely to succeed, the other one promising (Ed O'Bannon's class action lawsuit against the NCAA).

Not so obvious as a source of dangers is the continuing growth of service functions such as campus security and information technology. That growth has been associated with the employment of a host of non-academic staff. What do they do? Are they necessary to the effective management of academic institutions? Do they draw resources away from the accomplishment of the academic mission? Do they play a necessary, but often unappreciated, supportive role in its accomplishment? Are they sometimes a source of corruption? Examples are presented. Questions are addressed. Answers are offered, hopefully viable ones.

Near the end of this small volume, we return to the critical roles of the university president and the deans of the faculties. They are the institution's central leaders. They are the repositories of the academic mission, along with the tenured and tenure-track faculty. As they are effective, their institutions flourish. As they are found wanting, their institutions wane, weaken, and face the possibility of a slow death. Intermixed is the fate of faculty, students, and staff, whose livelihoods and futures are inextricably involved. How are these leaders appointed? How are they retired or—possibly—fired?

Higher education is under stress, but we believe the stress is manageable. So long as society remains free, we are optimistic that the integrity of the academic mission will survive. So long as curiosity is unfettered and creativity remains alive, while thinking and dialogue remain academic norms, the mission will survive. So long as academicians and society at large remain scandalized by corrupt sports programs, and awareness of the dangers lurking within the academic body is alive, the institution will continue to enrich society at large.

We extend public appreciation to those who have aided and advised us. In particular, we thank William Dill, former president of Babson College, as well as Matthew Gee and Raesean R. Paul, whose computer skills made the completion of the work easier. Appreciation must be given also to Mardrianna D. Campbell, whose devoted care makes it possible for the older author to continue a productive life. Any shortcomings in the book are attributable to the authors alone.

Abraham L. Gitlow,
Dean Emeritus and Professor of Economics Emeritus,
Stern School of Business, New York University

Howard S. Gitlow,
Professor of Management Science,
Fellow, American Society for Quality,
Director, Institute for Quality Management,
School of Business, University of Miami

Chapter 1

Higher Education in a Free Society

A. The Academic and Employability Missions

America's universities and colleges are admired worldwide for their freedom of inquiry and scientific productivity, but they face daunting challenges. Some of them are relatively recent; others are old and persistent in nature. The most profound of these challenges derives from their basic academic mission in the larger society. That mission is tripartite in nature, embracing: (1) the transmission of existing knowledge, i.e. teaching; (2) extending the boundaries of existing knowledge, i.e. research; and (3) the development of a capacity for critical thinking in student minds, and the exercise of that capacity by the faculty. Rene Descartes wrote centuries ago: "I think, therefore I am." A substantial part of America's higher education institutions perform also the mission of preparing students for employability, e.g. professional schools and programs in medicine, law, business, education, etc. These schools and programs, when built on a solid base of liberal arts and sciences, are not in conflict with the academic mission and ideal. When more narrowly constructed, their students' mind-set in analytical thinking may be weakened, and their future progress in both career and social settings thereby hampered. It is worth noting that university and college presidents believe that both academic and employability missions are well served by their institutions. Employers, on the other hand, have a contrary opinion with respect to the employability mission.

It must be explicitly understood and accepted that teaching shuns indoctrination, which is the enemy of science as it seeks to build blind acceptance of dogma. It must also be explicitly understood and accepted that research must be impartial, objective, and freely available. It must not be bought and paid for, in efforts to fabricate research to uphold predetermined conclusions, no matter how great the temptation. Finally, and most important, it must develop the capacity for inquiring minds to seek evidence as the basis for conclusions, and conclusions must be based on logical and rigorous analysis, that is replicable and unsullied by bias. These three aspects of the academic mission comprise its core values. They can often prove uncomfortable as they question a society's culture as handed down by posterity. Examples would be equality of the sexes in Saudi Arabia, or political democracy in China.

The central role and responsibility of higher education in a free society is to seek "truth," elusive and frustrating as that goal may be. Further, "truth," once discovered, must be treated as possibly temporary (i.e., the scientific method), and subject to change as research and inquiry unfold and discover new and different truths. That may be discomfiting, but it is a cost of freedom—and progress in teaching, research, and the development of critical thinking. These are the activities that are central as universities and colleges pursue their mission and strategy. In former times, those activities were conducted in collegiums, physical campuses that housed a community of scholars and their students. Those communities were characterized by an ethos, a set of values that emphasized the importance of evidence and civil discourse; and by a set of moral standards that, although often breached, still remained the ideal and touchstone of academic life. Now, that ideal is confronted by externally funded research that may create conflicts of interest involving a researcher's obligation to his or her university and its governance. The ideal may be challenged also by for-profit universities that were expanding exponentially, until checked in recent years by scandals in recruiting, and consequent government scrutiny and regulation. The for-profit universities relied heavily on online technology as their primary method of transmitting knowledge. Confronted by financial pressures, our non-profit universities and colleges, particularly the public institutions, are themselves turning increasingly to online teaching, with consequences as yet unforeseen to the traditional classroom, and its interaction between faculty and students. Then MOOCs (massive, open, online, courses) erupted, and further complicated the picture. Its proponents saw it as revolutionizing higher education. Serious debate grew around this issue, and it may turn out that online technology and MOOCs are not the panaceas their proponents thought them to be.

The core values underlying the academic mission suffer stress also because of the diffusion of power inherent in the nature of collegiums and the pressure on administrative authority to make and implement sometimes unpleasant decisions. With authority and power diffused over boards of trustees, administrative leaders (principally presidents, deans of faculty, and department chairs), and tenure-track faculty, effective governance becomes a problem. Woe to the administrator who arouses the ire of the tenured faculty. It has power over curricula, appointment, promotion, and tenure decisions. Prominent university presidents, let alone deans, have been brought down by outraged faculty. We explore the multi-faceted challenges inherent in this diffusion of power, including such matters as a sense of inequity among contingent faculty and their inclination to organize into unions. We consider also the problem of decision-making in a context of such crises as financial or academic paradigm change, when academics face the uncertainty of loss or impairment of their livelihood, and unpalatable decisions are necessary for institutional survival. In such a context, formal administrative authority may have to be exercised. Albeit a departure from the consensus ideal of the Academy, that approach is easy to understand: unpleasant decisions that may involve individual loss for faculty are unlikely to emerge from committees comprised of the individuals subject to that threat.

Because there is diffusion of power, authority must seek, through cooperation and university-wide optimization, to achieve a collegial consensus between administrators and faculty.

Underlying authority and its exercise lies a body of ethical principles. These principles are inherent in the creation and distribution of knowledge. They guide judgment about conduct in the intellectual sphere, and they set moral limits to action above those required by law. The ethics of knowledge define rules of conduct for the effective advancement of knowledge, undergird the integrity of faculty in relating to students, and of scholars in relating to other scholars. To fulfill these principles, according to Clark Kerr, the following actions are obligatory:[1]

- Careful collection and use of data, including the search for "inconvenient facts"

    Intelligent decision-making requires knowledge of the facts (realities), including those that are unpleasant and sometimes contrary to one's own opinions. An unwillingness to gather all relevant data can result in decisions that don't recognize reality. In most cases, it is a poor and dangerous academician who throws out inconvenient data.

- Careful use and citation of the ideas and work of other scholars

Wisdom dictates giving recognition and appropriate credit to all who contribute to the decision-making process. An important result is usually appreciation and loyalty—sentiments possessing incalculable worth. Leaders who take credit for everything that turns out well and assign blame to underlings for everything that turns out badly are not only unpopular, they are likely to become objects of scorn. More significantly, they provoke organizational problems that will overwhelm them and culminate in their "resignation" (discharge).

- Obligation to be impartial and skeptical

Biases and preconceived opinions are barriers to accurate assessment of reality, the key to good decision making. It follows that there must be consideration of alternative theories and their explanations of data. It is vital that there be complete freedom of expression (academic freedom) and tolerance of other viewpoints. Skepticism is healthy, because it makes it more difficult for facile and glib suggestions to win quick and easy acceptance, by submitting them to tests of evidence and probing questions. Civility in discourse with reliance on discussion rather than on coercion is important. Courtesy and civil discourse are imperatives for constructive discussion. Anger, impatience, and arrogance are anathema to productive interaction among academics, as they are with non-academics. Under any normal circumstance, coercion is counter-productive. After all, it rests upon the authority conveyed by formal status of office, rather than upon the authority growing out of reasoned persuasion (charisma or expertise). The latter is the coin of the academic realm.

- Open access for all interested in the research funding, methods, data, and analysis conducted within the Academy

Transparency is fundamental to pure scientific endeavor. It is the antidote for conflicts of interest that might color and distort research procedures and results. It is the ideal. But we know that the ideal is too often ignored. This happens when external funding seeks predetermined results that reflect sponsor pressure rather than true findings. It happens, perhaps more innocently, when researchers are secretive about research methods and results, because they seek exclusive recognition that might bring a Nobel nomination.

- Reliance on academic merit alone in evaluating the academic performances of others

  Personal feelings that reflect moral, political, and financial values must be separated from the presentation of evidence and analysis; as a corollary, personal feelings must be made explicit. (This calls for more transparency and candor than may have been practiced in the past).

- Care and consideration in handling human and animal subjects so as not to injure them unduly in the process of obtaining knowledge

  Problems in this area have led to the existence of Internal Review Boards (IRBs) and Health Insurance Portability and Accountability Act (HIPA) compliance requirements. Inadequate or perfunctory attention to the welfare of animal and human subjects of scientific experiments outrages the sensibility of well-organized, vocal, and influential groups. Their protests can hinder, and sometimes abort, research.

- Avoidance of making and advancing policy applications unless the full range of considerations entering into policy making have been carefully studied

  Under normal conditions, academic leaders should take time to allow complete consideration of all aspects of new or altered policies. This may require policy makers to become involved in the science of risk analysis: for example, Hazard Analysis. A deliberate pace allows full discussion and persuasion to enhance the likelihood of successful implementation of such policies.

- Following the general principle of "fair share"

  Participants are under obligation to cooperate carrying out their fair share of a team effort, as specified by the rules of the institution. This principle is vital in an age when scientific research is characteristically a team activity. Of course, the principal investigator, as team leader, receives appropriate recognition. But eventual success requires that other team members are dealt with in a respectful manner.

- Rejecting the use of position and facilities made available for the creation and transmission of knowledge for the advancement of unrelated personal pecuniary or political goals or of ideological convictions

  To allow such improper use of an institution's status and/or facilities is a violation of academic ethics, and deserves a punitive response. Society affords special status to higher education institutions, and the Academy must not abuse that status by tolerating individuals who use their university connection to advance personal goals, whether pecuniary, political, or ideological.

- Full acceptance of the obligation to faithfully teach students, to carefully advise them, to fairly evaluate them, and to refrain from exploiting them in any way

  Faculty and academic administrators should never forget their fundamental obligation to stimulate student's minds. Grade inflation is a violation of this obligation, especially when student evaluations of professors become significant in decisions relating to tenure, promotion, and compensation. Arrangements that promise valid learning experiences, but are really designed to get cheap or free labor (pseudo-internships), are also taboo.

- Full acceptance of the obligation to academic colleagues to assist them with advice on their academic pursuits, particularly for junior colleagues

  This obligation involves mentoring, and it is especially important at the graduate level. Senior faculty are obligated to advise their juniors' research efforts, as well as publication of results. Advice about tenure track appointments, as well as other career opportunities, is also important. Mentoring is equally important in teaching institutions.

- Full acceptance of the obligation, within departments, to seek a reasonable balance of colleagues by age, subject matter, specialty, and analytical method

A reasonable balance is unquestionably desirable but not always readily achievable. Nonetheless, conscious efforts by senior faculty to achieve a balanced age profile in their department is vital to avoid bunching, which involves the danger of large group retirements within a brief time period. Similarly, concentrations of faculty by subject matter, specialty, and/or analytical method is to be avoided.

Clark Kerr summarizes:

> The validity and pertinence of the obligations that make up academic ethics have even wider applicability. Respect for evidence and for contrary opinion are qualities of mind that we need throughout the society, as we resist the terrible certainties and brutal simplifications of the fanatic, the doctrinaire, the bigot, and the demagogue.[2]

B. Sources of Power and their Relationship to the Mission

There are three sources of power in an organization or institution; formal status, knowledge, and charisma. Formal status and knowledge seem self-evident. Charisma may not be. It is defined in the Random House Dictionary of the English Language as "that special . . . personal quality that gives an individual influence or authority over large numbers of people."

Formal status conveys power in any hierarchical social arrangement, and such arrangements have characterized human societies for millennia. It should be no surprise, therefore, to recognize formal status as a source of power. We shall return to this later, when we discuss the loci of power in universities and colleges, and face the fact that the titles of president, provost, dean of faculty, and vice-president indicate the power inherent in formal status.

Knowledge has particular relevance as a source of power. It goes to the heart of the academic mission, i.e., to pass on existing knowledge, and to expand the boundaries of that knowledge. Although society at large contains people who resent superior knowledge, and resist its power to influence others, the core mission of the university makes resentment and resistance by those who are less informed unacceptable.

Charisma is more elusive as a source of power, but nonetheless real. It is a quality in those possessing it that attracts and inspires others to follow. It is a personality trait that creates an aura of leadership. Charisma embraces moral authority. Presidents and deans of faculty who are charismatic find enthusiastic followers in the faculty and alumni, as well as among the students. They are able to generate acceptance for their judgments and policies. And that is no small matter in the diffuse, shared power of an academic institution.

Clark Kerr observed that "civility in discourse, and reliance on discussion rather than on coercion" are central to the academic mission. Yet, we will maintain that a leader must also be decisive, especially under conditions of paradigm shift, when decisions are likely to be painful to colleagues, and no amount of discussion is likely to yield a popular consensus.

Think of a drastic drop in enrollments and tuition revenues, or a sudden and unanticipated cessation of governmental grants, which may require a sharp cutback in staff. Decisions like that are unlikely to come out of a faculty committee that may include people who are in fear of their own jobs being at risk. And in such cases, a dean or university president may be required to use the formal power of authority.

A further observation seems appropriate. Knowledge can restrain the use of power, but the use of power is not restrained by ignorance and bias. In fact, power is most evil when it is accompanied by ignorance and bias. If we assume that the academic world is characterized by knowledge, a very popular assumption among academics, then it follows that the unrestrained use of power is least likely in that environment and given that ethos. But, unhappily, that is not always the case, because knowledge does not preclude coexistence with bias, and bias is a virus that can, and too often does, vitiate knowledge. However, that is life! We hope that education will trump both ignorance and bias.

C. Online Learning and MOOCs as they Relate to the Mission: For-Profit Academic Institutions

A significant difference between private for-profit and nonprofit academic institutions used to be technology, i.e., the primary delivery systems through which they passed knowledge to students. Private for-profit institutions relied overwhelmingly on online communications, while the nonprofits relied on traditional classrooms and laboratories that involved instructors and students in live, physical proximity. The University of Phoenix, the largest for-profit institution, lists numerous so-called "campuses" (some 200), but cannot match the extensive complexes or campuses of traditional non-profit universities and colleges, with their imposing buildings that provide classrooms and laboratories, as well as housing for faculty and students. Such facilities, in addition to being expensive to construct and maintain, require considerable supportive services for security, food, and more.

Pressure to increase the "productivity" of the non-profit research universities became intense during the financial meltdown of 2008-2010. An obvious and attractive means was enlarged use of the Internet for online communication between teachers and students. Of particular importance in this connection was the "tsunami" of interest and activity accompanying the appearance and introduction of MOOCs (massive, open, online courses). Many perceived MOOCs to be an easy remedy for the high cost of traditional, campus-based, personally interactive higher education. Others saw in them a profound loss in higher education's ability to transfer and extend knowledge, as well as to stimulate critical thinking.

In its March 15, 2010 issue, *Business Week* asserted that, in the first decade of the twenty-first century, for-profit higher education had achieved an enrollment of 1.4 million students, and generated revenue of $26 billion. While those are omnibus figures, they indicate that the scent of profit was in the air. Further strong expansion was in prospect, according to *Business Week,* but was checked by scandals involving recruitment and retention of students, graduation rates, defaults on student loans, and a dismal placement record after graduation. Nonetheless, the University of Phoenix and Kaplan University, in particular, as well as other less prominent for-profit institutions, conducted extensive and vigorous publicity campaigns to promote their programs. Full page ads in *The Chronicle of Higher Education* and *The New York Times* Sunday section on Education Life illustrated the competitive campaign aimed at attracting new students, as well as many who had attended extension and continuing education programs operated by a number of universities and colleges. But, there was doubt about the substantive quality of the learning that resulted.

The May 3–10, 2010 issue of *Bloomberg Business Week* had a lengthy article on the subject titled "Hard-selling the Homeless" noting that Federal aid to students at for-profit institutions grew from $4.6 billion in 2000 to $26.5 billion in 2009. Further, 75 percent of the total revenue of for-profits, as a group, came from federal funds. At Phoenix, the proportion was 86% in 2009, up from 48% in 2001 (federal law sets a maximum of 90%). Cognizant of abuses of the federal student loan program by some for-profit institutions, the federal government announced new rules in mid-July 2010, to become effective in November, after a period for comment and possible modification. The new rules tied institutional eligibility to the debt-to-earnings ratios and repayment records of former students and graduates. Three categories were proposed: green, yellow, and red. Green category institutions would need at least 45 percent of their former students paying down the principal on their federal loans. Also, their graduates would need to have debt-to-earnings ratios of less than 8 percent of their total income or 20 percent of their discretionary income. Red category institutions would become ineligible for federal student loan funds if fewer than 35 percent of their former students were paying down the principal of their loans, while graduates would need to have a debt-to-earnings ratio above 12 percent of their total income and 30 percent of discretionary income. In-between, i.e., yellow category, institutions would be subject to limits on enrollment growth and be required to notify applicants and students that they might have difficulty repaying their loans. These regulatory steps altered profoundly the business model of the for-profit sector. G. Blumenstyk, writing for *The Chronicle of Higher Education,* stated:

> On top of all the forces now weighing against the for-profit-college industry—continued government scrutiny, falling enrollments—there's one that hasn't grabbed any headlines but has the potential to up-end some of the most visible players in the sector: robust and inventive competition. MOOCs for credit, new ventures like the competency-based degrees from Southern New Hampshire University's College for America, and online programs like the one the University of South Carolina is creating with its Palmetto College are some of the emerging ventures that now offer as much (or more) of the convenience and flexibility that were once for-profit colleges' chief selling point.

> By the end of 2013, at least 87 percent of the United States population will have the option of taking online courses from an in-state public or non-profit college. . . . progressive nonprofits—those active in online education, like Western Governors University and Liberty University—have been growing in enrollment by at least 15 percent a year since 2006, while for-profit colleges' online-only enrollments began to fall off sharply in 2008 and 2009. In many cases, those public and nonprofit options are far less expensive than the for-profits are.

The sector that was once a major disruptive force in higher education is itself being disrupted.[3]

Southern New Hampshire University is probably the prototype for the *private, not-for-profit* university or college.[4] It combines a traditional, campus-based university with an enrollment of 2,750 undergraduate students, with a College of Online and Continuing Education that has an enrollment of 25,000 undergraduate and graduate students. SNHU's online programs constitute one of the largest and fastest-growing operations at any not-for-profit university or college in the United States. The College's administration forecasts that revenue will reach $200 million in 2014— four times what it took in for 2010–2011. Its courses are standardized. They are designed by professors who are experts in the subject matter. But, they are taught by part-time, contingent instructors (typically paid $2,500 per course). There are no formal class meetings. Students read online materials or watch a video or lecture. Student-teacher interaction occurs through posts on a discussion board. SNHU's baccalaureate costs $38,000, not cheap, but carrying a degree from an accredited academic institution, with an established reputation.

That doubt led Carnegie Mellon University to convene a new council, i.e., The Global Learning Council of educators, researchers, and technology-company executives, to develop standards and best practices in online education.[5] The Global Learning Council, chaired by Carnegie Mellon's President, Subra Suresh, will also look for ways to leverage education technology resources and disseminate data in an education landscape marked by technological challenges. The Global Learning Council will rely on research from Carnegie Mellon and other sources to address these questions: What would be good standards in online learning? What metrics should be used? And what methods are most effective?

In mid-March 2014, ApprovedColleges.com reported that 3,311 institutions claimed to have online course offerings. Closer examination revealed that the real number was more like 1,243. *The Chronicle of Higher Education* observed that the lower number was explained: "in part because the definition of 'online' is 'overly ambiguous and broad,' and in part because an institution that has multiple campuses can count each as having online programs, even if the institution in fact has only a single online offering available to all its students." The report noted further, "American colleges now offer 17,374 online programs altogether, 29 percent of which are master's-degree programs, with bachelor's and certificate programs making up 23 percent each. Business and management programs are the most popular, at 29 percent of the total, followed by health and medicine programs (16 percent), education programs (14 percent), and information technology and computers (10 percent)."

The glowing optimism that characterized the for profit sector a few years ago has been supplanted by the gnawing distress of the present outlook. Adding to that distress is the competition coming from established non-profit universities. A particularly significant example is provided by *ranked* top flight Business Schools that now offer master's degree programs that combine online and on-campus experience. As of early July 2013, almost 2 dozen such programs have been announced and are operating. They include Carnegie-Mellon's $118,000 MBA, Georgetown's $68,000 Masters of Science in Finance, and the University of Maryland's $80,000 MBA. Typically, these programs combine online work with on-campus experience that provides an interactive, small class atmosphere. Some programs include a chance to work with an international company, and travel abroad to present their findings. We believe the for-profit sector will ultimately stabilize, and become an integral part of America's higher education landscape. But it will have to improve its record in student retention, graduation, and successful postgraduate earnings. Also, it will have to do more to "clean up its act." As of March 2014, four for-profit institutions were subject to active investigation or lawsuits by federal agencies (Corinthian Colleges, DeVry University, Education Management Corporation, and ITT). Excepting DeVry, the other three, plus Career Education Corporation, were being actively investigated by over 15 state attorneys general. Of 15 for-profit colleges, five were "clean" (American Public Colleges, Capella, Grand Canyon, National American University, and Strayer). This data was reported in *The Chronicle of Higher Education,* March 7, 2014.

Technological advances have spawned a vast explosion of college level courses. A significant portion of them are now available at no charge to students around the world. The free tuition offerings (MOOC, i.e. massive, open, online courses) are supplied by non-profit universities through a corporate, *profit-seeking* entity called Coursera, as well as edX (MIT and Harvard), Udacity, and Khan Academy, as well as others. In addition to expanding accessibility to higher education, we consider here the quality of MOOC courses in transmitting knowledge, and developing critical thinking. Whether MOOC courses will meet that test is an open and debated question.

Coursera was established by two Stanford University professors in 2002: Andrew Ng and Daphne Koller. Their aim, in addition to making college level courses available world-wide, was profit. Since they didn't charge tuition, they sought revenue through a combination of fee charges (certificates, placement, tutoring, sponsorship, etc.). Initially backed by venture capital, more recently they sought financing by traditional non-profit university investors, plus non-investor participating universities. The participating universities also supplied the course offerings necessary to the viability of the enterprise. As of July 2013, there were 83 universities participating; several of those universities have equity positions in Coursera. The original university participants embraced four of America's most prestigious universities: Stanford, University of Michigan, Princeton, and University of Pennsylvania. The academic standing of these institutions, undoubtedly, facilitated acceptance of the supplied courses. The academic bona fides of Coursera was enhanced further in March 2014, when Richard C. Levin, formerly president of Yale University, became its CEO. Levin had significant connections internationally, especially in China. Collectively, the 83 universities participating in Coursera are offering over 100 courses, to some 3.9 million students. They are doing so through MOOCs. As of March 2013, the American Council on Education had approved four courses for college credit; originally, five courses were approved, but one was subsequently dropped. The five courses that were originally approved are: "Introduction to Genetics and Evolution" and "Bioelectricity: A Quantitative Approach" from Duke University; "Pre-Calculus" and "Algebra" from the University of California–Irvine; and "Calculus: Single-Variable" from the University of Pennsylvania.[6]

Sebastian Thrun and David Stavens developed a MOOC—edX, in a Harvard-MIT joint venture to which each institution contributed $30 million. In the summer of 2012, they were joined by the University of California–Berkeley, creating a powerful triumvirate. Courses are offered in the English language to participating institutions through open-source software developed by edX. Those institutions are welcome to introduce similar offerings of their own. There are plans to allow them to offer their courses on the edX website. There also are plans for the ed/X platform to create online learning software that goes beyond videos of lectures to interactive experience. College credit is not provided upon course completion, but certificates of successful completion will be available for a fee. The design of a viable business model is under study. As of May 2013, edX announced that it increased its participating membership from 12 to 27 university partners. The 15 new members included: 5 in the US (including Cornell and Davidson College); 6 in Asia; 3 in Europe; and 1 in Australia. By 2013, edX announced that it was on track to financial sustainability.[7]

Udacity, which competes with Coursera, is a for-profit university created by Thrun and Stavens, together with Mike Sokolsky, a partner. As of February 2013, it offered 20 active courses, with the expectation that they would serve some 400,000 users. Udacity was financed by a venture capital firm, Charles River Ventures, plus $300,000 of Thrun's own money. In addition, Andreesen Horowitz, another venture capital firm, provided an additional $15 million in October 2012. All this activity suffered a severe blow when, at the end of November 2013, Sebastian Thrun announced that Udacity was giving up on MOOCs, and concentrating on vocational training in the future. He did so after a carefully monitored MOOC program by Udacity was tested at San Jose State University and found wanting. Thrun described the learning results as "lousy." No one could accuse him of mincing words.

Khan Academy is a non-profit educational website created by Salman Khan in 2006. It offers over 4,000 micro lectures, through video materials stored on You Tube. Available in 19 languages, including English, German, Spanish, French, Russian, Chinese, Hindi, and Arabic, it covers 17 subject areas, ranging from mathematics and medicine to economics and computer science. As of mid-March 2013, it had delivered over 240 million lessons.

Although MOOCs originated in Stanford University with the creation of Coursera, the company name, not that of Stanford, comes to mind when the subject of MOOCs comes up. Another MOOC company, Udacity, also with strong Stanford ties, comes to mind as well, when the subject is discussed. It appears that Stanford, one of America's most prestigious universities, feels slighted by the prominence of Coursera and Udacity. It seems concerned that its own "brand" in this new and presumably huge education market has gotten lost. Stanford has, consequently, activated a robust effort to capture a prominent role for itself. It will provide an open source alternative to help other institutions develop MOOCs apart from those proprietary companies. It created an Office of the Vice Provost for Online Learning in mid-2012. That office numbers 25 platform engineers, course designers, data researchers, and media producers. It also supervises a research section (the Lytics Lab) that analyzes the large amounts of data generated by Stanford's online courses.[8]

The Chronicle of Higher Education published, in March 2013, the results of a survey of faculty who participated in creating and teaching MOOC courses.[9] The surveyed professors were tenured, and members of the academic establishment; making their opinions especially significant.

- Asked: "Do you believe MOOCs could eventually reduce the cost of attaining a college degree at your institution?"

  ◆ Answered: 64 percent responded affirmatively (24 percent said significantly, and 40 percent marginally).

- Asked: "Do you believe MOOCs could eventually reduce the cost of attaining a college degree in general?"

  ◆ Answered: 86 percent responded affirmatively (45 percent said significantly, and 41 percent marginally).

- Asked: "Did teaching a MOOC cause you to divert time from other duties, such as research, committee service, or traditional teaching?

  ◆ Answered: 81 percent responded affirmatively (55 percent said yes, and 26 percent somewhat).

- Asked: "Overall, do you believe MOOCs are worth the hype?"

  ◆ Answered: 79 percent said yes, and 21 percent said no.

The survey response is positive, and strongly so. But, there is a jarring and contradictory note in the survey results.

- Asked: "Do you believe students who succeed in your MOOC deserve formal credit from your home institution?"

  ◆ Answered: 72 percent said no, and 28 percent said yes.

- Asked: "Do you believe your home institution will eventually grant formal credit to students who succeed in your MOOC?"

  ◆ Answered: 66 percent said no, and 34 percent said yes.

These latter responses reveal strong reservations. While those reservations may relate to the intellectual substance of the MOOC and/or the learning that the student takes away, as compared with traditional classroom experience, it might also reflect worry about its impact on the job security of the faculty; or both. Our judgment is that the MOOC is here to stay, and will have a significant impact on higher education, both domestically and internationally. But, the reservations are serious, and the ultimate outcome will probably reflect an evolution of MOOC content and delivery systems, in addition to the learning students take away. There is also the nagging and basic question of whether MOOC courses will carry degree-granting credit that is transferable to established degree-granting institutions. William G. Bowen, president emeritus of the Andrew W. Mellon Foundation and Princeton University, wrote these words of caution: "There is a real danger that the media frenzy associated with MOOCs will lead some colleges (and, especially, business-oriented members of their boards) to embrace too tightly the MOOC approach before it is adequately tested and found to be both sustainable and capable of delivering good learning outcomes for all kinds of students." He went on to add: "Uncertainties notwithstanding, it is clear to me that online systems have great potential. Vigorous efforts should be made to explore further uses of both the relatively simple systems that are proliferating all around us, often to good effect, and sophisticated systems that are still in their infancy—systems sure to improve over time."[10]

The initial surge of enthusiasm that accompanied the arrival of MOOCs has collided with skepticism about its effectiveness in advancing learning. Additionally, there are questions about its extending knowledge, and developing critical thinking. As of mid-May 2013, faculty at four research institutions (Duke, Amherst, San Jose State, and most notably, Harvard) had challenged the uncritical adoption of MOOCs. They denied explicitly that they were opposed to online learning and its underlying technology. Rather, they emphasized their insistence on having meaningful involvement in its adoption and implementation. At San Jose State, professors in the philosophy department refused to use material from an edX course taught by a famous Harvard University professor. Their reason, bluntly put, was concern that the administration of the California State University system intended to replace them with MOOCs, because it was an inexpensive substitute. At Duke, an undergraduate faculty council voted down a decision by the provost's office to offer small online courses for credit through 2U, a company that sells an online platform and support services to colleges. A letter to the student newspaper, signed by 75 professors, asserted that students would "watch recorded lectures and participate in sections via web cam—enjoying neither the advantages of self-paced learning nor the responsiveness of a professor who teaches to the passions and curiosities of students." Note should be made that 2U has developed fully online graduate programs for several high-profile universities since 2008, including Georgetown University and the University of Southern California. At Amherst, the faculty rejected an invitation to produce MOOCs through edX.[11] At Harvard, 58 professors in the Faculty of Arts & Sciences signed a letter to their dean requesting formal oversight over the MOOCs offered by that institution through edX (co-founded with MIT). They expressed concern over critical questions about the impact of edX's activities on the faculties of universities adopting MOOCs taught by other Harvard professors. They expressed concern also about the effect MOOCs would have on the higher education system as a whole. They may have had no less concern about the fact that Harvard had become so deeply involved with MOOCs before consulting with them. Jeff Neal, the dean's director of communications, responded that a new committee would not be formed. Instead, Dean Michael D. Smith would continue to work with the two existing Harvard faculty committees "to support innovation in teaching and learning and to promote ongoing dialogue and debate of these important issues."[12]

At American University, the provost, in a memorandum to the entire faculty and staff, reiterated a "moratorium" on MOOCs. The university is delaying action, while it drafts a policy on how it will use MOOCs. It is considering whether to pursue institutional partnerships with edX or Coursera, or allow professors to teach MOOCs on their own, or through Udacity or some other platform. The memo assured the faculty that American University would not pursue MOOCs before addressing issues such as faculty oversight and release time. The memo, drafted in consultation with the Faculty Senate, set limits on freelance faculty involvement with MOOCs. For example, professors may not teach full courses online; they may not engage in any online teaching that costs students money or results in a certificate or course credit; they may not engage in any grading or assessment activities; and they must tell their deans about any freelance online teaching job.[13]

The Georgia Institute of Technology, recently invited to become the 63rd member of the Association of American Universities (AAU), took a different path. It announced a low cost MOOC-like Master's degree program in computer science, with support from AT&T.[14] It will work with Udacity to offer online courses that students could complete to earn a graduate degree from the university. AT&T is donating $2 million to get the program started, and will play an active role in some courses, *if professors agree*, offering guest speakers or suggesting class projects. Courses will be free through Udacity's site, made up of video lectures and computer-graded homework assignments. Students who want credit or a degree will be required to apply for admission to the university and pay tuition. Those students will have access to teaching assistants, and, in some cases, have their assignments graded by people. The tuition, however, will be far below that for traditional students: $134 per credit as against the normal rates of $472 for in-state students and $1,139 for out-of-state students. The university and Udacity will split the tuition revenue, with 60 percent going to Georgia Tech and 40 percent to Udacity. The future of the program seems under a shadow, since Sebastian Thrun's announcement that Udacity was dropping its MOOC activity, and would concentrate on vocational training.

The University maintains that the new online program in computer science will "provide an educational experience no less rigorous than the on-campus format." Although the courses in computer science will be available free to anyone, anywhere in the world, degree-seeking students will be virtually separated from "open" students, to guarantee the rigor of the degree-granting program. Admission to the degree program will require a B.S. degree in computer science from an accredited institution or a related B.S. degree with a possible need to take and pass remedial courses. In addition, admission will require selection through a graduate admission committee. To further ensure rigor and quality, the program will be tested with a smaller student cohort before being expanded to larger enrollments. Also, the pilot program will offer only a subset of the on-campus curriculum, being expanded as more courses come online. The integrity of examinations will be ensured by being consistent with national proctoring standards. Georgia Tech has access to 4,500 physical proctoring sites, and will work with online proctoring institutions.

Given the large difference in tuition between the online and on-campus Masters of Science in Computer Science programs, one must ask why a student would choose to come to campus and pay more for a residential degree. The university explained that the existing on-campus program "will remain a special experience that is qualitatively different—in terms of student community, faculty interaction, and project and thesis offerings—from the online offering, *particularly for those students who wish to pursue a PhD in computer science.*" The university acknowledged further "that certain aspects of on-campus programs simply cannot be replicated at present through the massive online format. There will always be a premium value on close faculty-student interaction, the ability to work directly with fellow students in groups, and to perform hands-on research projects. . . ." To assert that there is no qualitative difference in the online and on campus programs, and then turn 180 degrees and point out such differences, leaves one in a quandary. Both assertions cannot be true; the on-campus program is qualitatively superior. This is not to say that the online program falls short of deserving to be recognized as a valid degree-granting program. Given the extensive requirements of the program, it appears valid, on its own terms. Skeptics raise another issue, i.e., AT&T's involvement. Will AT&T seek to use the program as a training and recruitment arrangement? If so, won't that compromise the program's academic integrity? In any case, Georgia Tech's experiment with MOOCs bears watching.

Whether MOOCs become an established part of higher education was well assessed by Sanjay Sarma, who leads MIT's MOOC efforts. Derek Bok, former president of Harvard University, also expressed a positive opinion. Sarma asked, rhetorically, why MIT is excited by MOOCs. He answered that the traditional lecture mode, which can be traced back a millennium to the founding of the University of Bologna in 1088, needed change. He saw online, MOOC style education, as freeing up classroom time. He believed the freed time would enhance those magic moments of learning and mentoring that happen when students and professors go beyond the lecture or the textbook, and "try on ideas for themselves." In short, he sees MOOCs as providing automated teaching tools that can be assigned as homework, and free up classroom time for interactive discussion.

Derek Bok observed:

> The emergence of . . . (MOOCs), enrolling huge numbers of students, is causing many prominent professors to take an interest in teaching online. . . . Technology changes the nature of teaching. . . . Developing an online course is a collaborative venture in which instructors work with technicians and media experts. Teaching . . . becomes less intuitive and more of a collective, deliberative activity. In addition,

technology can produce a record, not just of what instructors say, but of how students respond to questions and homework problems. As a result, professors can discover what material gives students difficulty and try to adjust their teaching accordingly.[15]

While traditional quizzes and exams also provide insight into student learning, Bok presumably believes that online technology will expand and improve that insight.

A concluding note of caution re MOOCs. A limited survey of 34,779 students world-wide, who took 24 courses offered by professors at the University of Pennsylvania on the Coursera platform, revealed that they were already well-educated people. The implication is that MOOCs attract a relatively limited number of students, and do not reach the huge numbers of potential students generally thought to provide the MOOC market. The survey went to students who had registered for a MOOC, and viewed at least one video lecture. Over 80 percent of the respondents had a two-or four-year degree, and 44 percent had some graduate education. The pattern held for foreign students as well as for American ones. In some foreign countries where MOOCs are popular, e.g. Brazil, China, India, Russia, and South Africa, 80 percent of MOOC students came from the wealthiest and best educated 6 percent of the population.[16]

The survey warrants no sweeping conclusion. It is too limited in scope. Also, it reflects only the experience of respondents. We do not know what proportion they were of those who received surveys, but failed to respond. But it does provide a sobering caution that should temper the euphoria that accompanied the original introduction of MOOCs.

Notes

1. Clark Kerr, with Marian L. Gade and Maureen Kawaoka, *Higher Education Cannot Escape History: Issues for the Twenty-First Century* (New York: SUNY Press, 1994), 71–72.

2. Ibid.

3. G. Blumenstyk, "Nonprofit Colleges Compete on For-Profits' Turf," *The Chronicle of Higher Education*, June 21, 2013, A3.

4. John Hechinger, "SNHU, A Little College That's a Giant Online," *Bloomberg Business Week*, May 9, 2013.

5. Megan O'Neil, "New Council to Develop Standards, Best Practices for Online Learning," *The Chronicle of Higher Education*, November 11, 2013, Wired Campus.

6. Steve Kolowich, "American Council on Education Recommends 5 MOOCs for Credit," *The Chronicle of Higher Education*, Technology, February 7, 2013.

7. ———, "How EdX Plans to Earn and Share Revenue From Free Online Courses," *The Chronicle of Higher Education*, March 1, 2013, A8.

8. ———, "With Open Platform Stanford Seeks to Reclaim MOOC Brand," *The Chronicle of Higher Education*, November 8, 2013.

9. "The Minds Behind the MOOCs," *The Chronicle of Higher Education*, Technology, March 18, 2013.

10. William G. Bowen, "Walk Deliberately, Don't Run, Toward Online Education," *The Chronicle of Higher Education*, Commentary, March 25, 2013.

11. Steve Kolowich," Faculty Backlash Grows Against Online Partnerships," *The Chronicle of Higher Education*, May 10, 2013, A3-A4.

12. ———, "Harvard Professors Call for Greater Oversight of MOOCs," *The Chronicle of Higher Education*, May 24, 2013, posted in Distance Education, MOOCs.

13. ———, "As MOOC Debate Simmers at San Jose State, American U. Calls a Halt," *The Chronicle of Higher Education*, Technology, May 9, 2013.

14. Jeffrey R. Young, "Georgia Tech to Offer a MOOC-Like Online Master's Degree, at Low Cost," *The Chronicle of Higher Education*, Technology, May 15, 2013.

15. Derek Bok, "We Must Prepare PhD Students for the Complicated Art of Teaching," *The Chronicle of Higher Education*, November 25, 2013, A37.

16. Steve Kolowich, "MOOCs are Reaching Only Privileged Learners Survey Finds," *The Chronicle of Higher Education*, November 20, 2013, Wired Campus.

Chapter 2

Formal Authority and Diffusion of Power

A. Moral Power and Implementing Decisions

Morality and power are often taken to be opposites, with morality grounded in altruism and a commitment to the common good, and power located in self-interest. Our contention is that moral power, seemingly an oxymoron, is actually a widely present and important factor in social and political life. Moral power is the degree to which an actor, by virtue of his or her perceived moral stature, is able to persuade others to adopt a particular belief or take a particular course of action. We argue that moral power is a function of whether one is perceived as morally well-intentioned, morally capable, and whether one has moral standing to speak to an issue.[1]

Moral Power and diplomacy are two of the bases of successful management. But there is another element that must not be overlooked, especially in the cultural milieu of the Academy. It is an appeal to a fair, equitable application of those instruments to and by the faculty who inhabit the institution. In the Spring of 1966, during the course of his first budget meeting with the director of the university budget, one of the authors (who had just been elevated to dean from acting dean) had a noteworthy experience. Perhaps emboldened by that change in status—but he believes more by his sense of fairness—he had prepared his recommendations for faculty salary increases. Several considerations underlay his recommendations, namely, that they reward successful research output and possession of the doctorate, that they decompress the existing extreme clustering at the minimum salary levels for all professorial ranks, and that they alter cases of gross unfairness of treatment.

One such case stood out above all others. The dean was shocked when he first learned of this clustering and especially of the case of a long-service full professor, with over thirty years of service, who had been serving as chairman of the Economics Department. He had served as acting chairman for several years before being finally made chairman, never with any complaint on his part. He was a faithful, loyal faculty member, who accepted any and every call made upon him. He was also a gentle soul, unable to confront those who treated him without any sign of respect. But he was not a successful researcher, although he was a competent, but not inspiring, teacher. His salary was only $500 dollars per annum above the minimum of $12,000 for full professors. Remember, we are talking about some forty-seven years ago, before the inflationary period that marked the Vietnam War and the years immediately following. The dean submitted a 20 percent salary increase for him, to bring his salary to $15,000. The man's name began with the letter *A*, and so was first on the salary recommendation list. Also, the school was in very serious financial difficulty at the time. But the dean was convinced that his recommendations were vital to the success of his efforts to transform the school.

The director of the budget opened the meeting by moving immediately to the dean's salary recommendations. Of course, Dr. A's name was the item to be discussed. The budget director questioned the amount of the salary increase, criticizing it as completely out of line with the financial realities. The dean "exploded" asking how the director could be so unmindful of Dr. A's record of faithful service, and acceptance of the clear exploitation of him which had taken place over so many years. The dean remarked that he would be unable to go home and sleep that night if that exploitation was not remedied. He added that it was only the financial situation that kept him from recommending a significantly larger salary increase. Reflecting on the incident many years later, the dean guesses that the director of the budget had never before experienced such a strong reaction from a dean. The result was that the director said, "Don't get so excited." At which point, the dean said: "OK, Do you want to try another?" And that was the end of the budget review. The director simply accepted the entire package, and that was that. The story is not an example that can be applied by others without an accurate assessment of the human beings actually involved in the situation. But it is an example of the success that can attend a judicious mixture of courage, rectitude, and equitableness in human relationships.

B. Power Centers

Earlier, we explored the underlying ethos of the intellectual community, that is, the Academy, as well as its inherent drive to make decisions through civil discourse, and consensus. We considered also whether decision-making power (formal authority) played a role in that context, especially under crisis conditions (financial or paradigm shifts in the academic mission of the institution, e.g., a shift from a teaching emphasis to a research emphasis). It is appropriate to start with these observations by Clark Kerr, one of America's keenest and most experienced university administrators. In 1994, he wrote:

> [T]he university . . . has been given by most societies most of the time an exceptional degree of autonomy to conduct its own affairs . . . Given autonomy, the university has proven itself to be a highly conservative institution about its own affairs. The faculties are at the center of the enterprise. And, left to themselves, faculties make few changes. They rule largely to consensus, usually defer to their older members, and often subscribe to the view that colleagues should not raise controversial matters that may be divisive. All this conduces to the preservation of the status quo. By and large, students accept the functional authority of the faculty and, in any event, come and go relatively quickly. And administrators tend to be given little authority, and they also come and go. These two sources of potential change are usually quiescent.[2]

We will examine numerous tensions that characterize current academic life. Normally, they may be under wraps and quiescent. Yet, under conditions of financial stress such as prevailed in 2008–2009, hard decisions must be made. And consultation and discussion may not yield a consensus. When departments and/or schools may have to be terminated, the inner tensions can erupt and become a cauldron of adversarial and conflicting interests and opinions that harden and appear irreconcilable. At such a juncture, decision-making authority will be required, and will most likely fall to the key academic administrators. That is the moment that will test their administrative mettle, when decisions are made and implemented, unfortunately not by overall consensus, but by management fiat. And, especially in that context, numerical evidence (measures) may well be particularly useful in moving toward a consensus. Failing consensus, at least a widespread understanding of the urgency of the financial problem may be achieved. The importance of measurement extends beyond financial matters. It is significant also in exposing trends in enrollments, in the aggregate and more immediately in specific departments, as well as in such derivative concerns as tuition revenue and financial aid. There is also the spillover effect on faculty staffing and on housing for both faculty and students. And so it goes over the full panoply of tensions and administrative issues.

1. Board of Trustees

By law, the board of trustees is the repository of ultimate authority in the university. It has the power to hire or fire the president, and it usually has committees (nominating, budget, real estate, etc.) to advise and consult with the institution's administrative leaders on budgets and significant policy matters. For example, diplomas issued to graduates at commencement and other such times state that they are issued by the authority of the trustees, who have authorized the president and the appropriate dean of the faculty to grant the recipient all the privileges, honors, and rights customarily associated with the degree. Nevertheless, in the present age of presumed academic transparency, heaven help the trustee who seeks to exert pressure on academic affairs such as appointments, promotions, tenure, admissions, or graduation. Should it happen and become known, there would be outraged cries from faculty, no doubt accompanied by unwelcome publicity in the press.

A particularly egregious case illustrates the point. It involved the University of Illinois (Urbana-Champlain), Illinois' flagship and most prestigious public university. Originally reported in The *Chicago Tribune*, it caused Governor Patrick J. Quinn to appoint a special investigative panel to examine allegations that the university's admission decisions were influenced improperly by some trustees and state legislators. It was alleged that some 800 admitted students were on a list as having involved pressure by trustees and legislators. Those allegations claimed that an unspecified number of those admitted did not meet the minimum standards required by the university. The Better Government Association, an Illinois organization dedicated to improving government integrity and effectiveness, expressed no surprise given Illinois' unfortunate history of corruption, with the last two governors having left office indicted and disgraced. Eventually, the damage to the reputation of the university extended beyond Illinois. That happened because the story appeared subsequently in *The New York Times*.[3]

The ultimate tragedy of this sort of external pressure is that it frequently harms the very person who presumably benefits from the influence, namely, the student. The reason is simple. Such students are unprepared for the academic rigor that they will confront when classes begin, and can suffer failure, with all the psychological damage thereby inflicted. That damage can, unhappily, have life-long consequences. In any case, the publicity had an impact. Although he denied any wrongdoing, the chairman of the university's board of trustees, Mr. Niranjan S. Shah, resigned. His letter of resignation to Gov. Patrick J. Quinn stated that his action reflected his belief that the Governor's Special Investigative Panel wished the current trustees to step down. He added, "I am not in public service for self-aggrandizement and therefore have no interest in a protracted process regarding my role."

Several days later, the investigative panel issued its report. The report found the allegations to be accurate, and cited an e-mail in which a dean supported the admission of an unqualified student, stating flatly that this rejection might offend a major donor. There were numerous other instances of corruption, and the panel found a widespread climate of malfeasance in the board and the top administration of the university. One might well ask: Why would anyone want to be a university trustee, when there is implicit legal liability should negligence or conflict of interest occur in the exercise of trustee responsibility, or such damaging publicity if one seeks to exercise improper influence? Because the position carries considerable social cachet—it is seen as honorific. And our culture puts a premium on such a position.

That being the case, one can appropriately ask this question: What motives are in play when a university extends an invitation to someone to become a trustee? There are at least three motives, and they are easily understood. The first is to add luster to the institution by constituting a board composed of outstanding leaders of the community—people of major accomplishment in business, the professions, the arts, and also academe. The second is to gain a source of funds, either through major personal gifts and/or obtaining major gifts from others. The third is to benefit from the advice of such outstanding leaders. All three motives are important. But the second one (fundraising) can be a pregnant source of misunderstanding. It can create an impression that university trustee-

ships are for sale and can overwhelm the other two motives. The reality
is that not all wealthy prospects will be invited to become trustees. The
impression that the institution is "selling" trusteeships is anathema to the
ethos of academe. Nonetheless, the fund-raising motive is real and is
important to the long run financial health of the institution. Expert advisory input is also important, especially in the many supportive, non-
academic functions of a research university (budgets, finance and investments, real estate and housing, and so forth). There is a danger in the
advisory aspect of trustee participation in the university's operations: the
possibility of conflicts of interest. The problem arises when a trustee,
even with untainted motives, arranges for the university to do business
with a company in which that trustee, a close relative or a close friend,
has an interest. Although the relationship may be innocent the perception
can be troublesome. It is possible also, though we do not know, that
some believed that their business contacts were helpful to the university,
even if some private profit was made.

According to the folklore of NYU, some half century ago there was
a moment of institutional truth that profoundly affected its board of trustees. It involved the fund-raising aspect of the board. At that point in the
university's history, it was almost entirely reliant on tuition revenue to
support its operations. Although it had a lovely, small campus at University Heights in the Bronx that housed the University College of Arts and
Sciences and the School of Engineering, its operations were scattered
around Manhattan, with major locations at Washington Square, in Green-
wich Village, and on First Avenue, between 30th and 34th Streets, where
the Medical School was located adjacent to New York City's Bellevue
Hospital. The Dental School was nearby, on First Avenue near 25th
Street. The Graduate School of Business Administration was located down-
town, on Church Street, close to the financial hub of Wall Street. And
the newly-established School of the Arts was housed in an old structure
on the East Side, at Second Avenue, near 6th or 7th Street. These dispar-
ate locations had almost no housing for faculty and students, leading
some to describe the university as a commuter school.

Now, more than half a century later, the picture is radically different, and vastly improved, as befits one of our nation's leading universities and colleges, known and respected both domestically and abroad.
The Heights campus is gone, sold to the city, and now home to Bronx
Community College. The University College was merged with the Washington Square College of Arts and Sciences, becoming a single under-

graduate school at Washington Square. The Graduate School of Business Administration(now merged with the old School of Commerce and known as the Stern School of Business) and the School of the Arts (now the Tisch School of the Arts) are also now moved to Washington Square. There exists today a true university center at Washington Square, with extensive faculty and student housing, and outlying, new facilities on Third Avenue and on 14th Street.

NYU is now a residential university with an urban campus centered on historic Washington Square Park. The extraordinary physical and academic transformation described above involved very large sums, which were not generated from the traditional tuition revenues that had for so long sustained the old NYU. The money came from extensive, intensive, and continuing fund-raising activity, as well as long-term bonds that had to be paid off over time. It was at times a risky and hair-raising undertaking. But it has been a success, in significant part because of the role of the university's trustees. A university which had almost no significant endowment fifty years ago, now has one that exceeds $1 billion. But NYU's trustees of a half century ago did not see themselves in such a role. We cannot say for certain, but it seemed that their attitude was that their membership on the board was sufficient, by itself, to enlarge the reputation of the institution, and that no further real effort was needed.

In 1962, James McNaughton Hester was installed as president; he was youthful and ambitious for his new charge. Soon after taking office, he discovered Henry Heald's master plan for the future of NYU (which was published in 1956). Heald had gone from NYU's presidency to become CEO of the Ford Foundation. Under his leadership, the Foundation had begun making $25 million matching grants to select universities that promised to make academic breakthroughs with that seed money. NYU received one of those grants, and the rest is history. Seizing the opportunity and understanding the critical importance of vigorous fundraising, President Hester invited an alumnus who had retired after a successful career as an accountant and business entrepreneur, to help him in fundraising. That alumnus was a graduate of the School of Commerce, and he had raised money to help finance a new student housing facility at Washington Square, as well as money for the Dental School.

President Hester asked him to speak to the assembled trustees about the importance of fundraising, and how they could help in that effort. The alumnus agreed. But he was a somewhat curmudgeonly character, given to blunt and biting language, an aspect of the matter that the president may not have fully appreciated (but who knows). The alum came to the meeting with the trustees, and spoke somewhat as follows:

> Gentlemen (there were no female trustees, as we recall), if any of you has the idea that you bring honor to NYU by being a trustee, then you are wrong. NYU conveys honor on you by admitting you to its board, and with that honor, comes a serious obligation. It is for you to personally make substantial monetary gifts to the university, as well as working actively to help in bringing others to do the same. If any of you are uncomfortable with that obligation, then you have no business being here. You should resign, and make room for those who have a clearer understanding of their responsibilities as a trustee of NYU.

It was a bombshell. Some trustees were outraged; others were embarrassed. But those who were outraged shortly resigned. The others changed the nature of their role in the university along the lines put so bluntly to them by the alumnus. Of course, the alumnus never became a trustee himself, but if this apocryphal story is true, his contribution to his alma mater is beyond measure.

2. The President

The president is the chief executive officer of the university or college. She or he is the institution's leader, with all the implied organizational authority. Once installed, presidents are, theoretically, answerable only to the board. But as we have pointed out already, the true extent of presidential authority will depend ultimately upon leadership skills, the degree to which, by consultation, intellectuality and persuasiveness, plus psychological acumen, that officer leads the community of scholars who are his or her colleagues. The executive's most important attribute is probably the ability to articulate the institution's mission statement and strategy so as to capture the attention and support of the academic community, as well as the larger world outside. It is certain that the president's relationship with the board is critical. Indeed, a strong president will command the respect and support of the board. The larger world includes various constituencies whose support will be highly important to the institution. Of course, financial support is a key element. In public universities and colleges the state government—i.e., the governor and the legislature—plays a vital role. In private institutions, tuition revenue and fundraising are vital. In both types of institutions major grants, and increasingly, fundraising to build endowments, are critical. Endowment income took a significant hit in the fall and winter of 2008–2009. But over the long-run, it serves as an essential cushion against severe drops in other major sources of funds. We will discuss the president's role and responsibility in some detail, in the penultimate chapter.

3. The Dean of Faculty

The dean of faculty is a key figure in the institution's organizational structure. We will here abstract a few major aspects of the job.

First, consider the title itself: a dean of faculty has a specific constituency (the faculty of a college or other major academic division of the university, e.g., arts and sciences, law, medicine, dentistry, business administration, public administration, music, architecture, social work, education, engineering, and so on). The dean is that faculty's leader, with administrative authority to review departmental recommendations— usually transmitted to the dean's office by departmental chairpersons— concerning such fundamental matters as curriculum, number and variety of courses offered, numbers of sections scheduled for specific courses, promotions, tenure, hiring and other staffing matters having budgetary implications, and compensation. While the authority is real, the manner of its exercise can vary widely, from autocratic to highly democratic and consultative.

Second, consider the mission and strategy of the dean of faculty. A wise dean understands the nuances, and adopts an administrative style that encourages the faculty to buy into her or his mission and strategy for the school. Ideally, it also fits into the president's mission and strategy for the university. But suppose the president has not articulated a clear mission and strategy that embraces the entire university. Then an alert, innovative, and entrepreneurial dean can pursue his or her own mission and strategy for the school, and, over time, lead the university itself to adopt a new academic paradigm. Such a dean will leave an outsized imprint on the institution.

Third, consider that the dean of faculty is the interface between the school's faculty and the central administration (e.g., president, provost, and so on), the board of trustees, and the university's other deans of faculty. The third point resonates with potential issues, in particular the relationship with other deans of faculty and central administration. Usually, the key issue will involve budgetary matters (e.g., overhead charges placed on a school for central services, and balance of trade formulas where students take courses across school lines). A dean who acquires great skill as a negotiator can have enormously increased effectiveness in behalf of the school and faculty served. But there is a danger here. Skill that is too sharply and competitively exercised can harm the university as a whole, by generating resentment or envy, and become counterproductive.

Fourth, consider that the dean is a key figure for the students enrolled in that school. The dean whose signature will be affixed to every graduate's diploma is likely to be remembered by alumni—a consideration when that dean undertakes responsibility for that active fundraising which, as we have noted before, is an important role and constitutes a fifth aspect of the job. There are other significant constituencies that the dean must relate to, and that set of relationships constitutes the sixth part of the job: with alumni, with foreign or other domestic schools and universities, with government agencies and with other external groups.

From a managerial viewpoint, the role of the dean of faculty is almost as important as that of the president. Unlike vice-presidents or other officers of the central administration, the dean has a power base as the leader of a school's faculty. She or he will also typically have a constituency in her or his school's alumni body, and also possible representation on the board of trustees. A member of the central administration, even occasionally the president, is well-advised to think twice before confronting a powerful dean on an issue of major importance to that dean's school. It is equally true that a well-advised dean will think more than twice before entering into direct confrontation with the institution's president.

The dean's job calls for great diplomatic skill, as well as strong resolve, because there may be powerful forces that pull the university apart rather than unite it. In the case of NYU's old School of Commerce, there was considerable faculty and alumni opposition to the university's decision to raise the academic standards of the institution by changing from an essentially open admission school, with a highly practical "how to do" curriculum, to a far more intellectually rigorous, analytical, and theoretical curriculum. There was a drawn-out struggle before the outcome was clear. Fortunately for the school and the university, the change was hugely successful. But it took a resolute dean with a cadre of dedicated and supportive faculty to bring about that outcome. While deans do not win these confrontations solely by their resoluteness, they play a key role in winning the necessary faculty support. Their formal authority is enhanced and buttressed by charisma and knowledge.

Deans have another interesting challenge. They must transcend the use of their particular disciplines as the only lenses through which to view the Academy in general, and their college or school in particular. An over-arching, inclusive perception of the several disciplines that collectively comprise the intellectual entity of each college or school is vital, and can help promote collegiality, civility, and discourse among its members. Each dean must recognize and understand the value of all disciplinary perspectives present in his or her unit. For example, in a school of business there are several lenses for viewing the world: economics, marketing, statistics, accounting-finance, and so on. All the foregoing comments apply even more forcefully to the institution's president, who must mesh the several constituencies into a cohesive entity.

We should note that the title *dean* is also applied to some other administrative jobs in a university, depending on the particular practice in the individual institution, e.g., dean of admissions, but those titles are non-academic and do not carry the responsibilities and authority of the dean of faculty. Usually, business services and budgetary matters for the entire institution will be under non-academic vice presidents or directors. However, in some institutions, a director may actually head an academic unit, e.g., the director of the Courant Institute of Mathematical Sciences at NYU.

4. The Faculty Senate and Faculty Councils

The University of South Carolina–Columbia, founded in 1801, provides a clear example of an empowered Faculty Senate. Without any equivocation or qualification, the University's Faculty Handbook states:

> The University Faculty has legislative power in all matters pertaining to standards of admission, registration, requirements for and granting of earned degrees, curriculum, instruction, research, extracurricular activities, discipline of students, educational policies and standards of the university, and all other matters pertaining to the conduct of faculty affairs, including the discipline of their own members. The Faculty Senate of the University of South Carolina, having been created by direction of the University Faculty to act by and for that body, is endowed with all the powers and authority of the University Faculty except for those powers specifically reserved by that body to itself,

provided that the University Faculty may amend or repeal any general policy decisions adopted by the Faculty Senate.

The scope of the Faculty Senate's power is reflected in its ten committees: admissions, curricula and courses, scholastic standards and petitions, advisory, budget, grievance, steering, welfare, athletics advisory, and intellectual property. Its power is buttressed further by a University Committee on Tenure and Promotions, a Faculty-Board of Trustees Liaison Committee, and a Faculty Representative to the Board of Trustees. It is important to note that the Faculty Senate's membership is restricted to voting members of the faculty; and voting members are defined as full-time faculty holding the rank of Assistant Professor or above and professional librarians. The numerical composition of the body consists of ten percent of the voting members of each college or school. Presumably, each college or school's senators would work with their respective deans, carrying shared governance to their home constituency.

The existence of an Athletics Advisory Committee is noteworthy, implying a watchful faculty eye over sports programs. The language of the Faculty Handbook describes the committee's purview: "The committee shall review and monitor admissions decisions and the academic performance of all student-athletes by regularly receiving appropriate and relevant information regarding the academic eligibility and progress of student-athletes, including graduation rates." The language couldn't be clearer or stronger. Sadly, it didn't conform with reality. USC-Columbia is a big-time football powerhouse. Average attendance at home football games numbers 80,000, and alumni and other donors have contributed over $100 million in the last three years for athletic scholarships and athletic facilities. Given such enthusiasm, it is no mystery that some fans offered improper inducements to student athletes. In 2005 and 2012, USC-Columbia was held in violation of NCAA rules (note the repetition of infractions) and sanctioned with a small loss of athletic scholarships (six over two years in 2012, plus being placed on probation). Plainly, more than words on paper is needed to convert intention into reality. More on this subject in Chapter 7.

An alternative organizational structure would be a University Senate, which would include deans of faculty, administrators, and students, as well as faculty. Each constituency would be a Council and would elect a member as chair who would be regarded as representative and spokesman of its group. The Faculty Council would usually include full-time, tenure-track faculty from the several colleges and schools composing the university. Faculty Senators would normally communicate with their respective deans about school affairs. The chair of the Faculty Council would be in communication with the university president and/or provost. There might also be some interaction between faculty senators and members of the board, although it might not be formal. In addition, governance of the institution would be shared.

5. Chairpersons

Department chairpersons possess some formal authority, as they handle departmental budgets, course offerings and number of sections scheduled, secretarial staff, graduate student teaching assistants, adjunct faculty appointments, office allocations, and other more mundane matters. Of course, tradition governs, and tenure-track appointments, promotions, tenure decisions, compensation, curriculum, and other major concerns will be decided by the department's tenured faculty, with some input from tenure-track, but as yet untenured, faculty. The actual degree of decision-making power exercised by chairpersons will vary with the personal leadership ability of respective chairpersons, as well as with the character of the tenured members of the department. Some department heads feel that their role is simply as a representative of the faculty to the dean, which eschews any exercise of authority. But others will see themselves as a part of the school's administration, and will seek to influence (lead) the decisions arrived at by the faculty. They will exercise a more dynamic administrative posture, as they seek to "direct" the decisions of the department's tenured professors. Diplomacy and persuasiveness are key elements in determining effectiveness, and department heads, no less than deans, are well advised to remember that principle.

6. Legal Counsel

We are mindful of making sweeping statements about societal changes, but it does seem clear that America has become an exceptionally litigious nation. While it may be an overstatement, complaints about the frequency and scale of lawsuits, especially class action suits against large corporate entities, including universities and colleges, are no longer uncommon. We discuss three issues requiring legal counsel: privacy rights, conduct codes, and "town and gown." Of course, there are many other issues requiring legal counsel.

Grand plans to expand campuses, particularly those in urban locations, invite and engender legal actions designed to forestall them. At the least, they delay and make more expensive their implementation. In response, universities and colleges find it prudent, even necessary, to have an in-house legal staff, or to retain outside counsel. The role of the legal staff has become institutionalized to the degree that there is now a National Association of College and University Attorneys, with headquarters in Washington, DC. It was established in 1960–61, the dawn of a tumultuous time in America that confronted academic institutions with many legal issues. NACUA's membership consists primarily of non-profit colleges and universities in the United States, Canada, and some other foreign institutions. These institutions are represented by a primary attorney (presumably an in-house attorney), as well as additional attorney representatives. There are also arrangements for Associate Institutional memberships. The Association publishes relevant material, offers continuing legal education, and maintains a clearinghouse for attorneys to share resources, experiences, and work products on current legal issues.

a. Privacy Codes

Various legal issues complicate the contemporary academic scene. They arise in connection with present-day behavior and speech codes adopted by universities to accommodate the sensitivities of students and faculty, e.g., sexual harassment and date-rape allegations, as well as allegations of discrimination based on sex, race, or other grounds. In cases involving student allegations of sexual harassment by faculty, the institution has an ethical obligation to protect the rights of the faculty member, as well as those of the student—not a comfortable or easy position, but an important one, requiring wisdom as well as legal expertise. Then there are parents who are eager to know about the academic progress, or failure, of their offspring. But if the students involved are of age, they have privacy rights that preclude the institution from divulging the facts to their parents, minus their consent. How should deans, presidents, or other key academic leaders handle such situations? One thing is certain: they will want the advice of legal counsel.

b. Conduct Codes

An enthusiastic rush by academic leaders and faculty to support a presumed victim, and punish alleged perpetrators, can be deadly for the institution, as well as the involved deans, presidents, and faculty members. One need only recall the sad case of Duke University, where a female was invited to a fraternity house party by members of the university's lacrosse team. Subsequently, she alleged that several members of the team had raped her. The local district attorney jumped eagerly into action in behalf of the supposed victim, initiated a hurried investigation, and announced that evidence supported the woman. He followed with an indictment of three alleged perpetrators, and actions against them that could result in criminal convictions and the likelihood of severe punishment with jail sentences. Concurrently, the nation's media exploded with lurid accounts of the alleged crime. And Duke University's faculty and academic leaders, not all, but more than enough, joined the parade. They condemned the defendants before the case was tried in court. And the students were expelled, terminating their academic careers at Duke. Fortunately, the students' families were not poor, and they mounted a strong legal defense, led by competent attorneys. They launched an intense investigation into the background of the supposed victim, and perhaps more important, into the district attorney's own earlier investigation.

The outcome was astonishing, in light of the general rush to condemn the student athletes. It became clear that the alleged victim was unreliable, and her allegations did not hold up when scrutinized carefully. More telling, and a result of the disclosures resulting from the investigation by the defendants' attorneys, it became clear that the district attorney's investigation had doctored and falsified details of events. The result for that miscreant was that he was subsequently driven from office, disbarred, and then withdrew in disgrace. Duke University, along with the faculty and academic leaders who joined them, suffered a grievous "black eye." All around, it was a lesson in hastiness to be politically correct that ended badly. But it provides a cautionary example for the academic community.

c. Town and Gown

It is common for a natural tension to exist between a university or college (gown) and the community it resides in (town). Typical tensions in the view of the community include students driving too fast and students making noise. Common tensions in the view of the university include the community's desire for the campus to be a quiet park, or the community's putting up impediments (in the form of zoning regulations and/or building permits) that hamper and delay expansion and improvement of the campus and its buildings. All of these issues may have legal ramifications that need to be addressed by an institutional general counsel. It is significant that they arise, in one form or another, in urban universities and colleges as well as so-called "university towns." We note that both university administrators and local community officials have become more understanding and cooperative in recent years. Perhaps a significant reason is economic: universities are usually important employers of local labor, as well as a source of business for local stores and restaurants. Also, the presence of an academic institution tends to upgrade the ambience and make valuable services available to the local population. Given the desirability of an academic presence, cooperation by local officials seems logical. But there are other aspects: expansion of the university or college can upset a neighborhood, and rowdy students can disturb the local citizenry. The university also needs cooperation from local zoning boards, police, and so on.

These factors often result in the creation by an academic institution of an office or department of university communications, with a unit devoted specifically to community affairs. An office of communications (community affairs) can provide communications, marketing, and public relations services that advance the academic mission, as well as the institution's reputation and identity. Through its communications to the media and in the print and electronic materials it produces, it is able to disseminate information about its programs, research, and activities to both external and internal audiences.

Nonprofit academic institutions are free from local taxes, yet they require substantial services from local governments. Understandably, local officials and citizenry feel the resulting financial burden inequitable, despite the local business created by the institution. Over the years, a number of academic institutions have made arrangements to pay their host localities voluntary payments in lieu of taxes. Some of these arrangements were made many years ago, e.g., Harvard (1929), Princeton (the 1890s), and MIT (1928). Others are more recent: Brown (2004), Cornell (1968), University of California at Berkeley (2005), University of Minnesota-Twin Cities (not available), Notre Dame (2009), Pittsburgh

(2005), Virginia (1985), and Yale (1990). The payments ranged from Yale's high of $7.5 million and Harvard's $5.5 million, to Virginia's low of $151.5 thousand, with the others falling mostly between $1 million and $2 million. These eleven research universities indicated, in a survey of thirty leading institutions conducted by *The Chronicle of Higher Education*, that they made routine payments to their local governments.

The other nineteen universities indicated they made only occasional payments or other types of contributions. The bases for computing the payments varied widely, from Virginia's arrangement using the assessed value of the university's properties, multiplied by the locality's current real estate tax rate, to Yale's calculation based on the number of residence beds and the number of employees. Other arrangements were negotiated from what the university thought it could afford (Cornell), to annual adjustments calculated from a sum negotiated in the past (using the cost-of-living index, or some other measure). *The Chronicle* concluded, "Many of the nation's wealthiest institutions make no payments in lieu of taxes at all. Nearly two-thirds of the 30 research universities with large endowments surveyed . . . said they had no arrangements to make routine payments to their local governments."

The Wall Street Journal, in a relevant article entitled "Town and Gown: Why College Communities Look Smart,"[4] cited Professor Edward Glaeser of Harvard as having shown that when the proportion of a community's adult population with college degrees increases by 10%, wages in the community increase by about 8%. University-community interaction also encourages joint economic development projects, as well as internship opportunities for students. The article also described at some length the symbiotic relationship between West Virginia University and the community of Morgantown, where WVU is based. With an enrollment of 29,000, about the same size as Morgantown, the university and its hospital system employ almost 12,500 people, making it the largest employer in the state. In the period 2002–2007, when national economic growth annually averaged 1.1 percent, and state growth 0.7 percent, job growth in the Metropolitan Morgantown area averaged 3.2 percent. The entire West Virginia University system was estimated to have an annual economic impact on the state of $3.9 billion. The article told also of major building projects by the university that have had, and will have, huge impacts on the city of Morgantown, through strategic building in blighted neighborhoods that resulted in their redevelopment into attractive and desirable neighborhoods (no doubt with significant positive impact on property tax revenues for the city). Plainly, there are numerous areas of mutual interest and benefit in "town and gown" relationships. It would be foolhardy to allow instances of annoyance to cloud and undermine the benefits that cooperation produce.

C. Formal Authority and Diffusion of Power

We come now to a more detailed and specific consideration of the loci of power in academic institutions, and how it is exercised in an organizational context that is normally characterized by a diffusion of decision-making authority. The loci of authority are known and pretty well understood. They are the board of trustees, the university president or chancellor (both titles have been used to designate the institution's CEO), the several deans of faculty, chair people, and the tenure-track faculty. Depending on the president's conception of his/her role, there may be a provost to oversee internal operational management of the institution, while the president devotes time to important external relationships and constituencies, with special emphasis on major fundraising activities. Formal interactions of the president, the deans, and the tenure-track faculty often occur in a Faculty Senate, or some similar body. In some universities there may be a University Senate, but the power of this body, which would also include students and members of the university's administrative staff, is essentially consultative, not an integral part of the institution's decision-making structure—at least under normal circumstances. In crisis situations, fundamental decisions relating to restructuring the university, e.g., eliminating schools or colleges, changing pension and/or medical benefit plans, and so on, the University Senate's agreement to proposed courses of action may be sought. The Faculty Senate, however, would have power over academic matters.

D. The Challenge of Achieving Consensus

University leaders must be able to disseminate their mission statement, strategy, objectives, and metrics throughout the governance structure of the institution, in addition to those in the community and others with whom there is interaction, e.g., accreditation bodies. It is not always obvious how this goal is achieved. It seems reasonable to assume that all concerned parties would accept constructive ideas, but that is often not the reality.

Universities are unusual organizations in that portions of the work force have tenure, participate in governance, and are free to evaluate and dismiss any new ideas set forth by top management, under the umbrella of self-governance and "academic freedom." This is the context within which we consider effective communication, by which means leaders are able to spread their ideas more effectively, and achieve consensus.

Being human beings, with all the characteristics of the species, academicians do not necessarily evaluate new ideas relating to university purposes and operations on the basis of scientific studies. Rather, they depend on a subjective evaluation that emerges from collegial discussion. This is probably less true for scholarly research, where the emphasis is on objective evidence, and presumably the influence of subjective and emotional factors have less force. Of course, we have argued that objectivity and evidence are the hallmark of opinion formation in the academy. Unhappily, the reality falls somewhat short of that ideal, which is no reason to abandon the ideal, but which must somehow be managed by academic leaders in the here and now.

The key to winning acceptance of a new idea, e.g., an academic paradigm change, is for the administrative leader (president, dean, provost) to know and understand the faculty (the constituency). Every faculty, indeed every group of human beings, is characterized by heterogeneity in the ability and readiness of its individual members to adopt new ideas or organizational goals. There will always be individuals in an institution who are especially respected by their peers, have a network of contacts, and are role models for other members of their community. They are called opinion leaders, and they are the key transmission mechanism that the leader must enlist to win acceptance of his or her ideas and goals. Leaders seeking to diffuse an idea within a university need to obtain the commitment of the opinion leaders. They command such respect that their peers are inclined to view a new idea with favor, rather than remaining ensconced in the comfort of an existing and known mode.

If, despite the approach described, a new idea has failed of adoption, then what course of action is available to the administrative leader? Any further steps depend on the institutional circumstances of the university or college unit. When the context is one of institutional crisis, where a paradigm shift, either academic or operational, is necessary to continued viability and existence, the resistance must be overcome. But that is easier said than done. We believe the first place to look, in the face of failure, is the leader of the effort, i.e., the president or dean. Before condemning the faculty, examine the leader's management style and ability to articulate an idea. Actually, these characteristics should have been examined before his or her appointment, but sometimes a search committee fails either to assess correctly, or is fooled by a candidate's glibness. If, on re-examination and in the light of failure to produce the desired goal, the leader is found wanting, then his or her resignation should be demanded. If refused, discharge should ensue.

Consider, however, a leader who is competent, but sees a hard core of dissidents develop. It is assumed implicitly that the opinion leaders have been won over to acceptance of the need to adopt the new paradigm. There are a number of extrinsic, punitive actions that can be taken by an exercise of naked authority. But we do not recommend that course—certainly, not immediately. Rather, one should carefully review and assess each member of the resistant group, preferably starting with those among them who have emerged as leaders, even reluctant ones. Find those who are near retirement or who are burdened by illness, or some other condition that renders them susceptible to early buy-out agreements, and arrange attractive buy-outs that allow them to depart with dignity and reasonable financial security, or to find alternative employment opportunities more compatible with their academic capabilities (where terminal degrees are missing, or scholarly competence is not up to the standard required in a research university).

In this effort, the opinion leaders among the faculty are the academic leader's most potent allies. They are the key communication channel to spread the word about the arrangements that are available, and their desirability and respect for the prospective recipients. The proposed steps have been tested and found sound. The essence of the recommended approach is sensitivity and pragmatism, always free from displays of animosity. If a hard core remains, then, as a last resort, naked authority will have to be exercised, and resignations or discharges occur. In that event, good cause will have to exist as the basis of such harsh action. Without such cause, the remaining resistance will have to be dealt with as a disaffected and disorganized minority that time will take care of.

An excellent illustration of the points made above is provided by the case of Brooklyn College, a division of the City University of New York (CUNY).[5] The College is not a typical four year liberal Arts & Sciences institution. With an enrollment of 16,000 students, and individual departments that in combination (Finance, Accounting, and Business Management) approximate the enrollment of a substantial School (say 2,000 students), it is more akin to a university than it is to a college. President Karen Gould, pursuant to a plan to elevate the academic standards of the College, sought faculty approval of a common core of courses (Pathway). In particular, she sought to win accreditation from the Association for the Advancement of Collegiate Schools of Business (AACSB) for the combined business-related departments. AACSB accreditation standards require possession of doctoral degrees, records of research output by faculty, teaching load practices and the curriculum specified for the baccalaureate degree.

President Gould engaged in extensive consultation with the faculty and the department chairs. Several chairpersons disagreed with the proposed plans, as did some faculty. Specifically, the head of the Finance and Business Management Department, with the full support of his faculty, objected. President Gould, acting within the parameters of her administrative authority, dismissed him and other dissident chair people. The Finance and Business Management faculty filed a grievance (Brooklyn College has a faculty union, i.e., the Professional Staff Congress). President Gould agreed to consult with the faculty. An interim chairman supported by the faculty was appointed. The complaint was resolved, but the accreditation issue remained. The faculty appealed to the CUNY Board of Trustees. The Board indicated it would not intervene, commenting that President Gould's actions were well within her administrative authority. Given her extensive efforts to consult with the faculty, we come down on her side as she exerts the strength of naked administrative authority to effect academic progress in her College.

Notes

1. J. Mehta and C. Winship, *Moral Power,* Harvard University. See: http://scholar.harvard.edu/files/cwinship/files/moral_power-final_1.pdf.
2. Clark Kerr, with Marian L. Glade and Maureen Kawaoka, 72.
3. *The New York Times*, August 4, 2009, 14A.
4. *The Wall Street Journal*, March 24, 2009, 4D.
5. Neanda Salvaterra, "Brooklyn College Faculty is Riled Over Removals," *The Wall Street Journal*, July 20-21, 2013, A17-18.

Chapter 3

The Academic Pecking Order and Unionization of the Academic Staff

A. The Doctoral Degree and the Research Mission

American higher education has become obsessed with possession of the doctorate as the key to a full-time academic career. The unique hallmark of the doctorate is research which extends and advances understanding of our universe and our societies. And so research has become the unquestioned priority of the university. An apparently inevitable consequence has been the starving of the teaching obligation, and its subjugation to the needs of graduate, and most particularly, doctoral programs in universities. There is no conspiracy of silence in this connection. It is openly admitted that this is actually the prevailing situation. But there is a conspiracy of silence with respect to the actual management policies and practices that are used to generate surpluses at the undergraduate level that can be transferred to research and graduate programs. In four-year colleges and universities without doctoral degree programs, the priority is reversed.

In universities, management accomplishes the alleged starvation at the undergraduate level through staffing policies that generate excess funds for internal transfer to graduate and doctoral programs. Recruitment criteria and policies, promotion and tenure policies, and compensation practices all join to achieve the academic prestige and concomitant position which enhance fund-raising success and attract large numbers of students, swelling tuition revenues. Among the unhappy consequences arising from the foregoing bundle of policies and practices is a deep tension between teaching and research faculty. There is a sense of deep inequity which is corrosive to collegiality. We believe this is harmful to the teaching obligation to society through its creation of an internal class structure in higher education.[1]

Before World War II, teaching was the "bread and butter" activity in universities, as it was in four-year colleges. Research was largely uncompensated in any direct way (except, presumably, as it might be recognized in promotion, tenure, and salary decisions). Given the importance of teaching, even if it did not rank as high in academic prestige, it had to be weighed prominently in those decisions. Logan Wilson reported that at the University of Chicago the average professor spent 41.6% of his time teaching, 24.6% in research without special compensation, 12.7% for departmental services, 5.4% for administration, 4.5% for extra-mural activities without compensation, and the remaining time for other activities.[2]

Following World War II, and on into the 1950s and 1960s, there were many changes. Funding for research increased dramatically, and this resulted in changes at many universities, colleges, and other institutions. Many faculty members pursued an increased research agenda, with compensation. This was in line with the goals and objectives of their universities. Academia responded with reduced teaching loads for researchers, which in turn, created a need for increases in the number of faculty to accommodate the rapidly increasing numbers of students. That need was not accommodated, as we will see later, by increasing proportionately the number of tenure-track faculty. Rather, the employment of part-time contingent faculty was enlarged with some unhappy consequences.

Perhaps the most serious corrupting effect of external funding of research is the effort by some donors to control the direction and eventual publication of the research results. This danger is real and in profound conflict with the central value and purpose of research, viz., to be free to inquire and to explore without hindrance in quest of new knowledge. No less important is the freedom to publish what is discovered to other researchers, so that the intellectual interaction of lively minds can push the frontiers of knowledge even further. Both government (due to a desire by the military to protect the secrecy of new weapons, or concern over possible publication of critical evaluations of some agency) and private industry (due to a desire to protect patents, or to avoid publication of unfavorable research results that would impact badly on a market for a product) try to impose restrictions on the researchers.

We have no quarrel with the emphasis on research and the doctoral degree itself. At some point in our lives, each of us met the requirements for that seal of academic status from a university. We esteem the "calling" that it reflects. We do not wish to undermine its importance. In fact, we believe that it is appropriate as a necessary credential for teaching in colleges as well in universities. We value the intellectual capacity that it represents, and consider inherent inquisitiveness, sense of curiosity, and desire to pursue knowledge a critical necessity for effective teaching. But the sad fact is that not all fine researchers are also fine teachers, or that all fine teachers are also fine researchers. We call for a more balanced approach when we deal with promotion, tenure, compensation, and staffing policies and practices. We want, and we recommend, that academic managers at all levels, from president through to tenured faculty, recognize their obligation to society: to promote excellence in teaching as well in research.

B. The Teaching Mission

In the 2,675 colleges and universities in America in 2007, the major mission was teaching, rather than research.[3] This is not to say that research was unimportant in teaching. Keep in mind that research in one's field is important to effective teaching, because one must stay abreast of current developments. But teaching dominated the higher education landscape. The point is sharpened by the enrollment data. In 2007, there were 11.6 million undergraduate students in four-year colleges and universities. There were 2.3 million in universities offering graduate degrees (many without doctoral programs). Obviously, the largest segment was focused on teaching as the primary educational mission.

Institutions without doctoral programs are a heterogeneous universe, embracing a variety of educational foci. They include schools presenting themselves as universities since they offer masters' degree programs, coupled with their undergraduate divisions. These institutions will usually have several undergraduate schools, e.g., Arts & Sciences, Business, Education, etc. They include also four-year colleges that are primarily Arts & Sciences—like Lafayette or Franklin & Marshall—as well as those with undergraduate professional programs, like Skidmore (Business). Finally, there are institutions that are primarily professional, like Babson (Business). This multitude of institutions would require a separate volume, if it were to be examined in detail. Here, we simply observe that their major mission is teaching. Their size reflects the importance of that mission in higher education.

C. Staffing Profiles

It has become common at the most prestigious research universities, as well as those aspiring to greater academic stature, to organize undergraduate education into very large classes, with many smaller groups that meet with graduate teaching assistants. There is also a strong tendency to rely heavily on the use of adjunct and part-time instructors to staff the undergraduate courses. We think that this tendency has gone too far, and believe its main purpose is to substitute relatively inexpensive staffing for more expensive staffing (fulltime, tenure-track professors). A sad result has been the aforementioned sense of inequity and even exploitation, that has blossomed into efforts at unionization, engendering conflict, passion, and a significant departure from the reasoned dialogue that should prevail in the halls of learning. We will say more on this point later.

D. Academic Snobbery

Not all doctorates are equally prestigious. The PhD is the "King of the Hill." There are many other doctorates granted by universities, as well as by the private for-profit University of Phoenix, but they are simply not regarded so highly. They are usually granted in professional subject areas (e.g., DBA—Doctor of Business Administration, EdD—Doctor of Education, and many others). The differentiation is recognized in the reference to the more prestigious ones as the "higher doctorates" (because even in the non-PhD doctorates there is a pecking order, i.e., the MD—Doctor of Medicine as against the EdD, and so on.) These differentiations are reflected in subtle, and sometimes not so subtle, attitudes among the faculty that can cause internal disaffection and strife. That conflict can then be further reflected in quarrels over curriculum, teaching loads, committee assignments, and so on, that tend to aggravate people and make decisions more difficult to achieve.

One cannot wish these things away; they reflect the realities of life, the most basic being that nature is characterized by variation. It has simply not bestowed everyone equally with intellectual or physical abilities, talents, and interests. We can love the principle of equality and insist on its application with respect to access to opportunity; but given opportunity, not everyone will be able to perform with equal effect. Differences in performance can be due either to the individuals or the systems in which the individuals exist, or both. And so life does not distribute rewards equally in the current paradigm. Those not rewarded may become disgruntled and contentious. These problems must be addressed within the context of a managerial paradigm. When those unhappy with the results lash out and upset the effectiveness of an organization, then leadership is required to resolve the problems. And that is what the matter eventually comes down to. Absent such leadership, an organization will deteriorate, lose effectiveness, and eventually expire. An additional observation is that academic snobbery among faculty extends to inquiry, not only into the type of doctorate one has, but also what university issued it, and further still, what department and professor sponsored the candidate.

E. The Arts & Sciences and the Professional Schools

Historically and traditionally, the arts and sciences came to be regarded as the guardian of the Academy; it was virtual "calling," especially in the humanities. That is where the PhD degree originated and was housed. The arts and sciences faculty guarded their monopoly over the degree jealously and zealously, being loath to recognize its being awarded by any other schools/colleges, i.e., a professional school faculty. But in time, professional schools were established in research universities, and they wished to encourage and advance further knowledge in their fields. Their desire culminated in graduate research programs in the professional schools and their being given the right to grant doctoral degrees. Only slowly and over time were they permitted to grant the PhD, and some have not received that right to this day. It is futile for academic leaders to manage this pecking order by insisting on equal treatment for all doctorates, regardless of the real differences that do exist in their intellectual quality. It is necessary to reward their possessors with an eye to the competition within the Academy to recruit those having the more prestigious doctorates, as well as with an eye to external markets competing for their holders, e.g., business, government, and other.

Ideological fulmination that morality is outraged by inequality is overridden by the reality of market competition. While academic managers must work with that reality, we call for them to modify its harshness for the humanities by altering staffing profiles and establishing teaching loads to make possible an increase in the proportion of tenure-track, fulltime faculty. Some redistribution from faculty more favored by market conditions to those less favored is involved. But we think that inaction may prove far more painful in its long-term consequences for the Academy, and the values that we extolled and paraded as constituting the core of the Academy's ethos.

A further dimension of the foregoing tension is the never-ending difference over whether there should be undergraduate professional schools at all. For example, Harvard, Chicago, Stanford, and other prestigious research universities have only graduate schools of business, while at the University of Pennsylvania (Wharton) and New York University (Stern) there are also prestigious baccalaureate programs. Our position accepts the creation of such undergraduate schools, but on condition that their curricula incorporate a broad educational exposure to a core of science, mathematics, and the humanities, as well as to professional preparation by requiring courses that are analytical in nature and intellectually demanding.

To this point, we have not defined the content of the Arts & Sciences, i.e., the Arts and Social Sciences. The natural sciences, i.e. Physics, Chemistry, Biology, etc., are known, but the other subject areas are not widely or clearly identified. Yet we claim that they are at the core of a liberal education, and require administrative and faculty support and sustenance. We make this claim at a time after they have experienced a decline in student interest as well as perceived weakness as a basis for post-graduation employability. We refer to these fields of knowledge; Philosophy, History, Sociology, Political Science, Literature (The Great Books of Western Civilization, as well as those of other cultures), English, Foreign Languages, Anthropology, Basic Math (Algebra, Plane Geometry, Intermediate Algebra), and Economics. Only Economics is a sure breadwinner after receiving the baccalaureate. But their strength lies in their cultivation of the mind and its cognitive capacity. That is why we are so staunch in their defense as a solid base for success in later life.[4]

We have accepted so far the prevailing view that the proportion of undergraduate students taking majors in the humanities has suffered a drastic decline in the past four plus decades: from 17.4% in 1966 to 8% in 2007.[5] Michael Berube, who has outstanding credentials as an expert, (professor of literature at Pennsylvania State University and director of its Institute for the Arts & Humanities, as well as being a former president of the Modern Language Association) argues a contrary view, and asserts that the opposite is in fact the reality: the proportion taking humanities majors has held steady, moving slightly from 17.1% in 1970 to 17% in 2010.[6] How can this be? Both assertions cannot be correct. The answer to the question lies in how one defines the humanities. Professor Berube uses the definition of the National Center for Education Statistics. Its definition is very different and much broader than the one we have set down. It includes "area, ethnic, cultural, and gender studies; English language and literature/letters; foreign languages, literatures, and linguistics; liberal arts and sciences, general studies, and humanities; multi/interdisciplinary studies; theology and religious vocations, and visual and performing arts." The only common elements appear to be English and foreign languages and literature, liberal arts and sciences, and humanities. The rest embrace a huge range of study replete with popular and politically correct material. They produce a well-informed mind. But is it also a mind that is cognitively conditioned for critical thinking? As Hamlet famously said: "That is the question." For us, the narrower—and we think more rigorous—definition is the one that counts. Using that definition, there has been a decline in the proportion of students majoring in the humanities. But, it has stabilized at the 7.4 level, or somewhat higher. Of course, if one counts actual numbers, rather than proportions, the picture looks brighter.

F. The Power of Tenured and Tenure-Track Faculty

The nature and power of the American professoriate is reflected in its participation in the governance of the university.

The faculty of America's major universities has extraordinary privileges. Tenure is one of them, but perhaps not the most important. Few other professionals are able, with generous support, to do what they love best, and to do it in ways and on terms largely of their own making. Privileges of that kind call for corresponding responsibility, and the bonds that reinforce responsibility have frayed over the years.[7]

While they have frayed, they have not involved any lessening in the power of tenured professors over fundamental decisions regarding promotion, tenure, and compensation within their departments and schools, as well as the recruitment of newly authorized tenure-track professors.

Their willing participation in the exploitation of graduate teaching assistants and part-time faculty—discussed below in connection with the Yeshiva decision by the US Supreme Court—is ample testimony to the foregoing assertion. The faculty's power has been asserted dramatically also in the well-publicized resignations of Harvard's President Lawrence Summers and West Virginia's President Garrison. In the former case, there was controversy, first, over the allegedly nonacademic character of external activities by some members of the Afro-American Studies Department and, second, even greater disputation over some comments made by Summers in connection with a panel discussion of the relative scarcity of women in scientific research and academic departments devoted to it. In Garrison's case, there was the scandal related to the granting of an MBA degree to the daughter of the Governor of West Virginia, when she allegedly lacked the required credits for the degree. In that case, the president's resignation occurred despite his having procured the largest financial support on record from the State Legislature, as well as his having the strong and steadfast support of the University's Board of Trustees.

William H. Danforth, long-time Chancellor of Washington University in St. Louis, pointed out a risk to the integrity with which faculty carried out their responsibilities to the research and teaching missions of the Academy. He noted that many faculty members are focused on their disciplines and professional associations. This tendency has been magnified by the focus on outside resources and on an international reputation as a criterion for tenure. The loosening of institutional ties involves a significant risk because today's successful academic institution requires internal operations aimed at agreed-upon goals. The participation and leadership of faculty are a vital and essential element in achieving institutional success.

Since federal funds became available to fund research work having practical commercial applications, an important issue emerged. Can university-employed inventors assign their ownership rights to companies as part of consulting agreements? Stanford University, for example, tried to reclaim a series of patents that it lost due to such an employee agreement. A federal appeals court upheld the transfer to the company. A significant number of universities and the American Council on Education have asked the US Supreme Court to take up the case, arguing that the ruling clouds the universities "title to thousands of federally funded inventions, contrary to Congress's intent and the public interest."

University leaders must be sensitive to the possibly corrupting influ-ence of financial arrangements between research faculty and external sponsors. A compelling and dramatic case came to public attention late in May 2009. It involved the University of California-Los Angeles and one of its best neurosurgeons. The case was reported in *The Wall Street Journal*. As a result of a Congressional investigation, it was discovered that Dr. Jeffrey Wang, chief of spine surgery at UCLA, did not disclose that medical firms, whose products he was researching concurrently with their use in patients, were paying him for the research. During the period in question, 2004–2007 inclusive, he failed to report receipt of $459,500. California state law requires university researchers to reveal financial arrangements with private organizations that fund their research. Failure to reveal such arrangements exposes the delinquent researcher to civil liability and university discipline. In Dr. Wang's case, UCLA and the doctor declined to comment when the news became public.

In any case, several legislators accused a number of universities of being lax in overseeing conflicts of interest. Presumably, their concern reflected worry that payments to doctors by medical device manufactur-ers and drug companies would influence the research results, and com-promise their accuracy and integrity. Maine, Massachusetts, Minnesota, Vermont, and West Virginia have all passed laws that require medical companies to reveal payment to in-state physicians, with some excep-tions. The seriousness of Dr. Wang's failure to disclose is magnified by his stature in the medical profession. Apart from the alleged violations of California law and internal UCLA policy, there is no allegation that Dr. Wang actually colored research findings, or harmed his patients. In-stead, the central problem is the inherent conflict of interest, and the grave potential for undermining the scientific integrity and value of the affected research.

Another—and more fundamental—problem is the inherent long-run threat to faculty retaining their precious and vital participation in univer-sity governance, along with their power over tenure, promotion, com-pensation, and recruitment of new tenure-track faculty. Presidents, pro-vosts, chancellors and deans are responsible for upholding and advancing the well-being of their institutions. If that responsibility collides with the growing loyalty of faculty to external institutions, then, from a manage-rial viewpoint, the leaders must act. We believe this and say it bluntly: action is what they would and should take. There is already considerable discussion, both within and outside academe, about tenure, with its usual life-long guarantee of job security. Comments are increasingly sharp that tenure, apart from its significance as a strengthener of freedom of expression by faculty, contributes to their lack of attention to their internal obligations as they pursue outside interests and remuneration.

More and more, there is pressure to withhold tenure from younger faculty in exchange for limited contracts of employment. If that tendency continues and grows stronger, then tenure will erode and the general rule of employment will metamorphose into something more akin to the industrial relations model. That would be an incalculable tragedy for faculty, and for the academic culture that is so important to the transmission and expansion of knowledge. More will be said about managing conflicts of interest in a later chapter.

The global financial crisis that shook America and the rest of the world in 2008 imposed unanticipated budgetary pressures on higher education. It suddenly created conditions calling for drastic emergency decisions affecting faculty recruitment and compensation, as well as structural rearrangements in academic programs. All are sensitive areas where faculty traditionally played major roles in decision-making, but in the context of a financial crisis, many academic administrators became more assertive in exercising decision-making authority, minus the traditional and more time-consuming procedures involving faculty consultation and consensus prior to decision and action. To put the matter mildly, faculty feathers were ruffled, and cries of outrage were difficult to mute or moderate.

G. The Empowered Faculty and Unionization

The US Supreme Court, in its 1980 landmark Yeshiva University decision, altered the academic landscape.[8] Despite their prized power over such academic decisions as those affecting tenure, promotion, compensation, and curriculum, tenure-track faculty did not have ultimate authority over university-wide decisions regarding general budgetary policies. And in the stressful inflationary environment prevailing in the United States in the seventies and early eighties of the twentieth century, there was probably a general sentiment among that powerful group of faculty that they were falling behind in compensation. That sentiment may have been buttressed by the annual salary surveys of *The Chronicle of Higher Education*, as well as by the restive and generally rebellious behavior on university campuses, typical of the turmoil that marked the sixties and the Vietnam War period.

In any case, there was an effort on some campuses to organize the faculty into unions. That effort brought the unionization effort to a boil at Yeshiva University in New York City. The Yeshiva University central administration fought the organization of its faculty, contending that they were not employees within the coverage of the National Labor Relations Act, and so the university was not obligated to recognize and bargain with the union. The National Labor Relations Board, the agency charged with enforcing the provisions of the law, upheld the union's claim that the faculty were indeed employees, and that the union was therefore entitled to recognition as its official bargaining agent. The case wended its way up through the federal courts, being appealed until it reached the Supreme Court. In a landmark 5-4 decision, the Court upheld the judgment of the Court of Appeals, and thereby upheld the position taken by Yeshiva University. Justices Powell, Stewart, Rehnquist, and Stevens, joined by Chief Justice Burger, constituted the majority, while Justices Brennan, White, Marshall, and Blackmun populated the minority. In crystal clear language, the majority wrote:

1. The authority structure of a university does not fit neatly into the statutory scheme, because authority in the typical 'mature' private university is divided between a central administration and one or more collegial bodies. The absence of explicit congressional direction does not preclude the Board from reaching any particular type of employment and the Board has approved the formation of bargaining units composed of faculty members on the ground that they are 'professional employees' under section 2(12) of the Act. Nevertheless professionals may be exempted from coverage under the judicially implied exclusion for 'managerial employees' when they are involved in developing and implementing employer policy. 2. Here . . . the controlling consideration is that the faculty exercises authority which in any other context unquestionably would be managerial, its authority in academic matters being absolute. . . . 3. The deference ordinarily due the Board's expertise does not require reversal of the Court of Appeals' decision. This Court respects the Board's expertise when its conclusions are rationally based on articulated facts and consistent with the Act, but here the Board's decision satisfies neither intention.

A particularly interesting case involved Rensselaer Polytechnic University in Troy, New York. The critical issue was the withdrawal of the university's recognition of the faculty senate's role in the governance of the institution. The university's drastic action followed the faculty senate's decision to admit non-tenured faculty and to give them voting rights in the faculty senate's decisions. Note must be taken of the existence of a unit of the American Federation of Teachers at RPI. The AFT is a union, and its membership is heavily weighted with elementary and secondary school teachers. We surmise—but do not know for a certainty—that the combination of those elements may have worried the RPI administration and board. Perhaps the continued recognition of the faculty senate, with its enlarged membership, might have led to RPI's being unable to claim exclusion from the obligation to bargain collectively with a faculty union under the logic of the Yeshiva decision.

In any case, RPI's administration announced in August 2007 that it would no longer recognize its faculty senate. The stated reason was that the faculty senate had amended its rules to allow voting by those who were not on the tenure track. Professors are still working to try to reconstitute the senate and regain recognition. The deeper significance of RPI's action is twofold: first, it will probably cause other tenured faculties to shun unionization, as well as any efforts to extend their traditional power to non-tenured faculty; and, second, it will encourage university administrators to include tenured faculty in decision making, to avoid dealing with faculty unions and the implicit threats of confrontation during contract negotiations.

It is important to note that the Yeshiva decision applies only to private universities, and thus excludes faculty in public universities, where they are covered under state statutes. Those laws may legally protect them in their right to organize into unions and bargain collectively. Nonetheless, that right may be weakened, due to the spillover influence of the Yeshiva decision, as well as the inherent cost-benefit calculations of the faculty as they contemplate the overall impact of unionization and collective bargaining on their power and status under the ruling ethos and tradition of the academic community. The essential point is that tenured faculty members are seen as a part of management, with significant power over economic as well as academic decision-making. And this perception is supported by a decision of the US Supreme Court. If unionization involves a substitution of the industrial relations labor-management relationship for the traditional participatory power of tenured faculty, as in the RPI case, then tenured faculty are unlikely to support that substitution. And that appears to be the outcome of the Yeshiva decision. The steam went out of the movement toward unionization of tenured faculty after 1980. But it continued to percolate among contingent faculty and graduate teaching assistants.

H. Contingent Faculty and Graduate Teaching Assistants

The power possessed by tenure-track, full-time faculty does not extend to part-time and adjunct faculty, or, perhaps more importantly, to graduate teaching assistants, whose status as to unionization and collective bargaining may have been settled temporarily in the case of Brown University (1-RC-21368).

The Brown decision, by a reconstituted and more conservative (3 Republicans and 2 Democrats) NLRB, revisited and overturned an earlier NLRB decision involving graduate students at NYU. That earlier Board decision (3 Democrats and 2 Republicans) had held that graduate teaching assistants at NYU were employees covered by the National Labor Relations Act, thereby compelling NYU to recognize their union and bargain collectively, resulting in a contract. The Brown decision reversed that finding, and, in effect, upheld the force of the Yeshiva decision in private research universities by extending it from tenured faculty to TAs. One result was the withering of the NYU graduate student union, following an unsuccessful strike. The composition of the NLRB changed again in 2010, to 3 Democrats and 1 Republican (1 seat remained open), when President Obama made two interim appointments of committed union protagonists to the Board (one of them is Craig Becker, a lawyer for the AFL-CIO and the Service Employees International Union). The Board, given a relevant case, might issue a ruling that overturns the Brown decision. NYU may well be that case, because, given the new composition of the NLRB, the university's graduate student union demanded in May 2010 that NYU should voluntarily recognize it. Failing such action by the university, the union took its case to the reconstituted NLRB. Controversy over the president's interim appointments kept the Board from any decisive action. But the matter may have been resolved by an NYU-UAW (United Auto Workers) agreement to put the unionization issue to a vote by the graduate student employees. To be held in December, 2013, with the vote supervised by the American Arbitration Association, a key part of the agreement was union acceptance of the exclusion of many research assistants from the vote, i.e., from unionization. The excluded RAs are: all employees at the university's NYU-Polytechnic division; those in the departments of Psychology, Mathematics, and the hard sciences; MBA students at the Stern School of Business; and graders, graduate assistants, and tutors at the Medical School. Although the union agreed to the exclusion of RAs in the hard sciences and engineering in the vote, it reserved the right to attempt their organization and participation in collective bargaining.[9]

The underlying and serious issue is whether the status of TAs as graduate students might conflict with the matters they might desire to bargain over, e.g., their right to take up allegedly unfair grading or thesis evaluations by faculty. An issue like that would really "put the fat in the fire." On the other hand, they have been exploited in their employment as low-paid teachers, especially in the undergraduate classes of prestigious universities and colleges, where low-cost staffing profiles help managers transfer funds from the undergraduate programs to the graduate and research ones. This exploitation is quietly accepted by tenure-track faculty, who may not even realize what is occurring, as a consequence of their pressure for reduced teaching loads and improved funding for their favorite research projects.

One consequence is a sense of inequity among graduate teaching assistants, who have perceived a possible major strengthening of their position through unionization and collective bargaining. At the end of the first decade of the twenty-first century, there exists pressure to organize, as well as resistance by managers and, frequently, by tenure-track faculty. It's certain that the cost-benefit assessment of organization is very different in the case of graduate teaching assistants from what it is among tenure-track professors. The case of part-time adjunct faculty is also unclear, as to the applicability of the labor relations law. However, in their case the cost-benefit assessment of organization is likely to be tempered by their desire to obtain full-time status, and move onto the tenure track, where they will then enjoy the privileges and the benefits that would thereby come to them.

These issues are discussed at length by Marc Bousquet, an openly anti-capitalist and powerful protagonist for adjunct faculty and graduate student unionization.[10] In fact, he wants unionization across-the-board, perceiving universities as having been co-opted by our capitalist, market- oriented system. In his view, the universities have been corrupted, and they can only be cleansed and redeemed by a strongly pro-active, powerful, and confrontational union movement. It is probably fair to say that, in that confrontation, he sees the tenured, senior faculty as an enemy, because their privileges and superior compensation are based on the "exploitation" of both the untenured, part-time faculty and the graduate students. It should be no mystery that Bousquet's views reflect most strongly the situation of graduate students and lower level faculty in the humanities, where external labor market conditions are least favorable, thereby exacerbating the "exploitation" problem.

While some analysts consider the underlying source of the "exploitation" problem to be an overproduction of PhDs, Bousquet denies that explanation as profoundly in error. He says the problem is a "manufactured" under-creation of jobs, reflecting the sharp reduction in the proportion of tenure-track faculty employed for teaching.[11] Bousquet goes on to charge that "cheap teaching is not a victimless crime." He argues that it affects all non-tenured faculty ranks and teachers. His bitterness and opposition to the prevailing order is reflected further in his charge that casualization is an issue of racial, gendered, and class justice, falling most heavily on minority, female, and untenured employees. Finally, he writes, "Late capitalism doesn't just happen to the university; the university makes late capitalism happen." In a foreword to Bousquet's book, Cary Nelson makes clear the meaning of his clarion call to the underclass of the academic universe to rise up and overcome the "exploitation" that is built into the existing system.[12] Nelson writes:

> Deny administrators the right to fund gratuitous pet projects at the expense of a principled campus salary schedule. If administrators refuse to comply, sit in their offices, sit in front of their cars, block campus streets, block access to buildings, picket their houses. Use nonviolent civil disobedience to force change. Or, if that seems too confrontational, form a union and negotiate these matters at the bargaining table. Increasingly, graduate employees and contingent faculty are doing just that. The key decisions about the job system are made on your own campus when budget priorities are set. Take the money in your own hands. You have nothing to lose but your colleagues' chains.

With that resounding paraphrase of Karl Marx's famous ending to *The Communist Manifesto*: "Workers of the world unite. You have nothing to lose but your chains," Nelson makes clear that he and Bousquet want to tear down the existing system.

We have acknowledged our own recognition of the existence of exploitation in the Academy. We have called for administrators and boards in private universities and colleges to be aware and alert to the threat that it poses, and to rearrange their priorities so that we return to older staffing patterns, and increase the proportion of classes, both undergraduate and graduate, that are taught by tenure-track faculty. This will pose a substantial budget problem, to which Bousquet and Nelson may be deliberately blind. To start, and being pragmatic, teaching loads of tenured faculty, which have declined significantly as the emphasis on research became a top priority, would probably have to be revisited and increased. The implication is that research productivity would not suffer severely, if at all, by such an increase. But, the affected faculty may well resist, and argue to the contrary. This is clearly an occasion to appeal to their sense of academic values, and an appreciation of what Veblen called the "civilizing" role of a proper undergraduate liberal arts education. It is also important to explain the threat to their pleasant present arrangements unless they act, both pragmatically and morally, before the deluge (to use a famous historic word uttered by a French monarch before the Revolution). Indeed, the sharp economic contraction of 2008–2009 has probably magnified the long-term problem, and made it even more difficult to correct. *The Chronicle of Higher Education* described the situation in these words:[13]

> With the economy as a backdrop, the report . . . spotlighted the plight of faculty members who work off the tenure track, in particular instructors who work part-time. The proportion of part-time and fulltime adjunct faculty members (including graduate assistants), a figure that the association closely tracks, grew from 43.2 percent of the professoriate in 1975 to 68.8 percent in 2007. The proportion of adjunct faculty members (excluding non-tenure track FT) who are part-timers rose from 30.2 percent to 50.3 percent during that same time period. In 2009, in public universities, 31 percent of the faculty were FT tenured (23%) and FT tenure track (8%); while 68 percent were off the tenure track (42 percent were graduate assistants). The overall picture was almost the same in private universities; 34 percent of the faculty were FT tenured (23%) and FT tenure track (11%); while 66 percent off the tenure track (but 22% were graduate assistants, 26% were PT adjuncts and 18% were FT adjuncts).

Unfortunately, the reversal in the proportion of full-time to part-time faculty is not accompanied by equivalent data on compensation. The *Chronicle's* Almanac Issue does not contain data for contingent faculty. John Curtis, director of research and public policy for the American Association of University Professors (AAUP) noted three obstacles that explain the situation: (1) the likelihood of inconsistent data (universities do not keep information on part-time faculty in a centralized location, as they do for full-time faculty); (2) the AAUP's data collection survey cannot be easily adapted to include part-time faculty compensation data (because the number of part-time faculty, the number of credit hours, and the rates of pay by credit hour or course would be needed to complete the calculations); and (3) the AAUP's research operation is not sufficiently staffed to enable it to gather this information. Clearly, the new majority faculty, i.e., those employed on contingent appointments, remains an afterthought in data collection.

Given this data deficiency, we must rely on our collective experience and other anecdotal evidence, when we assert, as do so many other observers, that contingent faculty are disadvantaged in the academy; and, unhappily, exploited. It is a festering sore which will get worse with time, unless academic leaders take timely steps to correct the situation. *The Chronicle of Higher Education* conducted a limited survey of twenty-five higher education institutions to get some idea of the steps being taken to handle the budgetary quandary they face in a severe economic downturn.[14] Ten are public universities and ten are private universities. The other five are community colleges, not relevant to our discussion.

The survey asked the universities to indicate whether they were, or were not, using these steps: (1) restricting or delaying faculty hiring; (2) freezing or cutting salaries; (3) increasing teaching loads; (4) restricting travel; (5) restricting adjunct/contingent hiring; and (6) other steps. Of the ten public universities, nine restricted or delayed faculty hiring; six froze or cut salaries; five increased teaching loads; five restricted travel; five restricted hiring of adjunct or contingent faculty; and five used furloughs. Only one cut tenure-track faculty numbers (the University of Florida). Of the ten private universities, nine restricted or delayed faculty hiring; nine froze or cut salaries; only one increased teaching loads; four restricted travel; only two restricted hiring of adjunct or contingent faculty; and one restricted sabbaticals while another cut the number of tenured and tenure-track faculty. The public institutions surveyed included (in addition to the University of Florida) Arizona State, The Citadel, Clemson, the University of Minnesota system, Utah State, the College of William and Mary, and some other schools. The private institutions surveyed included the faculties of arts and sciences at Dartmouth and Harvard, Johns Hopkins, Stanford, Vanderbilt, and several others.

Although the survey is limited and one should be cautious about drawing conclusions, we are struck by the greater readiness of the public institutions to increase teaching loads (five public as against one private). We are struck also that only one public and one private university cut the number of tenured and tenure-track faculty. The private institution is Spelman College, a relatively small institution compared with the University of Florida (the public university). Of course, that probably reflects the infinitely greater job security that attaches to tenure, as well as the fact that the tenured faculty is one of the major power centers in universities and colleges. In any case, the foregoing data indicate that increases in teaching loads are likely to be a tough hurdle for academic leaders to surmount. Yet that may be one of the paths that would help reverse the trend between adjunct, part-time, and graduate assistants relative to tenured and tenure-track faculty in the classroom and the laboratory. The initiative rests in the hands of academic leaders. We urge them to accept that leadership initiative, and at least start a serious review of faculty staffing profiles.

Notes

1. Robert Rosenzweig, *The Political University*, (Baltimore: Johns Hopkins University Press, 2001), 103–104.

2. Logan Wilson, *The Academic Man*, (New Brunswick, NJ: Transaction Publishers, 1995), 104.

3. Statistical Abstract of the United States: 2012, US Department of Commerce, Washington, DC, 2011, p, 178.

4. Lee Siegel, "Who Ruined the Humanities," *The Wall Street Journal*, July 13–14, 2013, C1, C2; Anthony T. Grafton and James Grossman, "The Humanities in Dubious Battle," *The Chronicle of Higher Education*, Views, July 5, 2013, A25, A26.

5. Michael Berube, "Consider This," *The Chronicle* Review, July 19, 2013, B4.

6. Ibid.

7. Rosenzweig, xv.

8. NLRB v. Yeshiva University, 444 US 672–1980. No. 78–857. Argued October 10, 1979, and decided February 20, 1980. Henceforth cited as NLRB v. Yeshiva.

9. Peter Schmidt, "Union Drive for Graduate Students at NYU Gets Go-Ahead," *The Chronicle of Higher Education*, Faculty, November 27, 2013.

10. Mark Bousquet, *How the University Works: Higher Education and the Low-Wage Nation*, New York University Press, New York and London, 2008.

11. Bousquet, 40–45.

12. Bousquet, xv–xvi.

13. *The Chronicle of Higher Education*, Almanac Issue, 2011–2012, August 26, 2011, 28.

14. *The Chronicle of Higher Education*, April 17, 2009, 11A.

Chapter 4

The Budgetary Challenge and Fiscal Responsibility

A. Importance

Budgets can be key indicators of institutional objectives, and of progress toward their achievement. But the data they present must be accurate and timely. Those criteria are not always satisfied. The university or college's data recording operations may be a mix of computer and manual recording procedures, and they may not be compatible. In such instances, the academic leader needs to take remedial action, which can be expensive and may engender resistance from personnel invested in the existing systems and procedures. Despite those hurdles, corrective action is critical so that meaningful and useable budget data is available—for analysis and planning, as well as for tracking progress. Without reliable data, the president and other leading administrators are blind to underlying problems, and at risk of blundering into decisions that are contrary to institutional needs. Expenditures, when unmonitored and uncontrolled, contribute to fiscal emergencies and delay or abort plans for academic progress.

Budgets also serve an analytical purpose, along with acting as a control on wasteful expenditure. The academic leader who is knowledgeable about budgets can discover from them relationships between various policies and their impact on revenues and expenditures. For example, a change in tuition policy, combined with a change in unfunded financial aid policy, will impact revenues and expenditures. An increase in tuition, coupled with a significant increase in unfunded financial aid, can fail to increase revenues if the latter action offsets the former. Similarly, teaching load and class size policies will affect staffing expenditures. Understanding the relationship is vital to the outcome. Clearly, planning is facilitated as is progress toward the achievement of institutional goals. These are matters of critical concern to presidents, deans, and other academic managers, who are responsible for the financial health of the institution.

B. Characteristics of a Financially Healthy University or College

Michael Shattock[1] described seven criteria that contribute to an academic institution's financial health. They are: (1) short term solvency; (2) retention of reserves; (3) effective management of long term debt; (4) effective management of plant and equipment; (5) generation of non-state funding; (6) consistency between the budget and the institution's strategy; and (7) constant effort to improve the efficiency and the effectiveness of operational procedures.

1. Short-Term Solvency

A solvent institution pays its obligations in a timely manner. Consequently, it does not need recurrent and frequent recourse to borrowing to continue operations. The danger of such borrowing is that lenders may suddenly refuse to continue providing funds, and precipitate a crisis. NYU faced such a situation in 1972, when its banks, fearful that the university would be unable to repay loans regularly provided to cover August payrolls, notified the university that such bridge loans would not be provided. NYU, which was heavily reliant on tuition revenue, needed the loans before the September term brought in tuition revenue. The banks had given the university notice early in the year. The university's emergency and ensuing major structural reorganizations were traumatic, and only narrowly enabled its survival, and subsequent extraordinary growth in reputation.

2. Retention of Reserves

A university or college must have sufficient reserves to withstand unexpected shifts in external funding, to respond opportunistically to events, and to recover from disasters (e.g., acts of God and terrorism). The

NYU case, just noted, illustrates how important the retention of adequate reserves can be. Budgets should be constructed with an eye to maintaining reasonable reserves.

3. Effective Management of Long-Term Debt

Universities and colleges use medium- to long-term borrowing for capital purposes. In a period of low inflation the interest rates are usually low, which encourages borrowing. But the capital repayment burden, plus interest, will be borne by successor administrative leaders in a period far ahead, when the state of the financial environment may well be very difficult. Examples of situations that can entice academic leaders to borrow are: (a) a donor who makes a pledge payable over time, usually of a substantial amount, but who wants immediate implementation of the building or program that she or he is interested in; (b) a donor who wants to "leverage" a donation by requiring that the university match the gift by raising an equal (or sometimes greater) sum from other sources, failing which the initial gift will be only partially forthcoming; or (c) a donation—usually for a program of some sort, as distinct from a building or part of a building (room, suite, lounge)—that is insufficient to endow the program into the future; i.e., it will not generate an income stream that will cover the anticipated annual costs of the program. Fundraisers, whether presidents and deans or professional fundraising staffs, are greatly tempted to do these things, being carried away by a desire to announce publicly any sizeable gift, as a sign of success in a fundraising drive. Academic leaders should shy away from this financial trap.

4. Effective Management of Plant and Equipment

Experience shows that building maintenance is frequently the first item on which academic institutions economize. Evidence from both the private and public sectors suggests that the mismanagement of capital assets often creates financial difficulties. In fact, one important indicator of an institution's financial health might be the magnitude of its long-term maintenance fund. We add the observation that faculty and staff are always eager to postpone maintenance in favor of improvements in compensation and benefits. However, when the roof begins to leak and building contents are damaged or ruined, raising the specter of imminent danger to life and limb from occupying unsafe structures, they are likely to be in the forefront of those clamoring for the heads of the administrators for their imprudence and lack of reasonable foresight.

5. Generation of Non-State Funding Sources

Shattock speaks here about public universities in particular, but the point has importance also for private institutions. The essential point is that too-heavy reliance on a single source of funding is financially perilous, because any sudden shift (shortfall) can produce a crisis. The financial crisis of 2008–2009 provides ample evidence of that fact. The University of California system is a leading case, as is the University of Arizona. During the financial crisis of 2008–2009, UA's reliance on state funding threatened major problems for the institution. The problem was rooted in the state's large budget shortfalls, coupled with the requirement that the state maintain a balanced budget. Many public universities and colleges found themselves in a similar situation, even if not so severe. In those cases, one action was to raise tuition on out-of-state students, who are, oddly, present in significant numbers in our so-called state universities. Originally, those institutions were established to provide higher education opportunities to state residents. But over time, and as ever-easier transportation enabled our population to become increasingly mobile, state universities accepted students from out-of-state, and even from other countries. They did so in the name of educating students for a world characterized by global and interdependent economic activity, as well as cross-cultural interaction.

6. Consistency Between the Budget and the Institutional Strategy

Academic institutions need to align their budgets with their mission and strategy, so that their resources are rationally allocated. For example, absent a strategically focused budget, distracting but attractive opportunities can present themselves, and undermine the mission of the institution. Well-intentioned projects for social or political benefit can sap the institution's resources, and misdirect organizational energy away from its mission and strategy. One of our colleagues was speaking with a vice president of information technology in 1988 about his university's strategic plan. The vice president of IT stated that he had just spent several million dollars on super computers. When the inquirer asked him why, he responded: "It was a strategic decision!" The colleague asked him where the institution's strategic plan discussed supercomputing as part of its strategy. He received an irritated look from the vice president of IT. In his opinion, the V.P. had just misspent valuable resources on a non-strategic issue.

7. Ability to Improve the Efficiency and Effectiveness of Critical Processes

The previous six characteristics comprise wise guidelines for creating and maintaining a healthy budget for a research university, as well as for all higher education institutions. To quote Albert Einstein: "We can't solve problems by using the same kind of thinking we used when we created them." And so it goes with research universities. Although the first six criteria help to keep research universities from getting into trouble, they are not sufficient to get universities out of it. The economic crisis of 2008–2009 provides an excellent case study. Imagine a research university that experienced a dramatic drop in its endowment, say 30 percent. The first six criteria by themselves cannot efficiently and effectively help the university's management cope with the decrease in operating revenue caused by the drop in endowment. What theory, methods or tools are available to the leadership of research universities to help them cope with such an economic crisis? The answer is improvement in the efficiency and effectiveness of critical processes. We are not talking about the lip-service type of process improvement that is pushed down through an organization with no behavioral change by leadership. Rather, we are speaking of the painful and powerfully effective process-improvement methods that require a paradigm shift in how financially troubled research universities function, and how their top managers behave.

C. Budgeting for the Future: The NYU Case

New York University's financial picture seemed to provide a good illustration of carefully planned budgeting and operational analysis.[2] We focus on NYU's plans for handling a budgetary shortfall of some $120 million anticipated in fiscal year 2010 (NYU's total annual budget amounted to some $2.6 billion). Pursuing improvement in its operations even before the financial crisis of 2008–2009, the university adopted a re-engineering program aimed at achieving greater efficiency and cost reductions. That program was expanded and intensified, and projected into future years. Some details will indicate the nature of the program.

First, there was an analysis of anticipated revenue shortfalls ($80.9 million) and anticipated additional costs ($39.1 million). Second, there was a list of savings targets to bring about budgetary balance.

This was no "pie in the sky" exercise. The anticipated revenue shortfalls included: (1) a reduction in endowment income of $33.2 million together with a reduction in philanthropic gifts of $17.6 million; and (2) an assortment of other items like a reduction in intended increases in tuition, an intended increase in financial aid, and so on. The anticipated cost increases included: (1) needed capital expenses of $13.6 million (new classrooms, wireless expansion, zoning costs); (2) needed university investments in school academic programs and in university-wide information technology services of $11.6 million, as well as additional costs for personnel, international student loans, and direct lending. The savings targets, by category, included: (1) zero percent salary increases for non-contract employees ($23 million); (2) university level administrative savings ($53 million, of which $38 million had already been achieved); (3) school level administrative savings ($38 million); and (4) spendable endowment fund balances ($6 million).

NYU's longer-term plans involved a dual approach: (1) steps that are essentially capable of being applied "across the board" for the entire university; and (2) steps that would require inter-school cooperation, or would otherwise involve more than one unit of the university, but not the entirety. The first approach identified sixteen items. Among them were : (a) freezing most external hiring (students and faculty exempted); (b) implementing voluntary 3- or 4-day work weeks at pro rata salaries for appropriate positions (health insurance and other benefits which are not salary-linked to be retained at full value; salary-based benefits to be pro-rated); (c) implementing mandatory 9-, 10-, and 11-month contracts at pro rata salaries for appropriate positions (benefits managed same as #2); (d) eliminating jobs (with prior approval); (e) reducing non-essential service (with prior approval); (f) freezing use of most temporary help (students excepted); (g) freezing all non-promotional administrative salary adjustments; (h) significantly reducing employment of consultants; (i) significantly reducing travel, entertainment, and car service spending; (j) booking of required travel with volume discounts whenever possible; (k) significantly reducing food service at internal meetings; (l) significantly reducing printed vs. web-distributed material; and so on.

The second approach identified seventeen items that would be given careful, thoughtful, and open-minded review. They could be bundled as involving outsourcing (e-mail services, components of advertising and publications, components of payroll services, and administration of defined benefit plans); consolidating (Provost and EVP budget offices, Office of Academic Appointments and Human Resources, Institutional Research and Strategic Assessment, Environmental Services and Operations); replacing computer labs with wireless lounges & collaboration software; renegotiating most service and supply contracts; reducing future benefits costs for new employees (in effect, creating a two-tier compensation system); and so on.

The highly pragmatic plan did not apply to selected vice presidents and the recruitment of top-flight professors who would add to the university's prestige as a research university. For this select and highly favored group, compensation arrangements were made involving, in some cases, millions of dollars through loans (later forgiven and not repaid).This actuality was not disclosed when the plan was made public. It became public during the Senate hearings on the confirmation of Jacob (Jack) Lew as President Obama's nominee for the office of Secretary of the Treasury. Mr. Lew had been a vice-president of NYU prior to his nomination. His compensation included, among other benefits, the purchase of a luxurious summer home on Long Island (involving approximately $1 million).

Republican opposition to the nomination was strong, and all aspects of Lew's employment by the university were investigated. The results were published by *The New York Times* in a series of unflattering articles. Martin Lipton, one of America's leading corporate attorneys and chairman of NYU's Board of Trustees, vigorously defended the university's and President Sexton's actions in a letter to *The Wall Street Journal*. That letter, terse and to the point, explained the arrangement as being necessary to and supportive of the effort to make firm the long-term effort to cement NYU's reputation as a first-class research institution. But at the university, there were many deaf ears and little "buy-in." Subsequent investigation revealed that such arrangements were not limited to Mr. Lew, but embraced a significantly larger group of favored recruits.

The ultimate outcome of the furor was an announcement that the policy of providing and forgiving loans for favored faculty and administrators would be terminated. NYU also announced that President Sexton would retire in 2016, when his term in office would expire. Pregnant with meaning was this concurrent statement by Martin Lipton: "No university can prosper if there's disruption, if there's unhappiness in the family." It appears that the power of the tenured and tenure-track faculty continues to be alive, and can be ignored only by presidents and boards that enjoy high risk behavior.[3]

There is another approach to handling budgetary shortfalls, especially when one believes they will be of relatively limited duration. It can be used along with the NYU plan's measures, made public for the benefit of the tenured and tenure-track faculty and non-faculty employees. Or, it can be relied upon as the major "tool" for financing such shortfalls. It involves borrowing, especially by issuing tax-free bonds that will provide immediate funds, but involve repayment over some future time period. A number of America's leading research universities used this approach to overcome the budgetary shortfalls of 2008–2009, and perhaps some years beyond. *The Wall Street Journal* described the situation.[4] Typically, long-term debt has been used to finance construction projects and other projects with a lengthy life. Unhappily, the 2008–2009 cash crunch impelled a number of America's top-rated universities to borrow long-term to obtain funds for current operating expenses. "Moody's counts 12 schools with double-A, or triple- A ratings that collectively have borrowed more than $6 billion in recent months to meet their regular obligations." Harvard University issued $1.5 billion in debt, while Princeton sold $1 billion. It is noteworthy that many of the universities with the largest endowments found themselves illiquid and needing cash for current operations. The reason was their heavy reliance on endowment income (20 to 40 percent of operating revenue) at a time when those endowments suffered severe losses (partly from investment strategies that magnified both gains during a boom and commensurate losses during a financial crisis).

While borrowing by issuing bonds takes care of immediate budgetary problems, it raises some longer-term hurdles for successor academic leaders. First, it may simply postpone needed strategic and operational problems, e.g., grandiose institutional objectives, and/or operational inefficiencies. Second, the need to pay off the principal and interest on the additional debt will burden the institution's future budgets. Third, in the event of future increases in interest rates, the repayment burden can grow beyond the level originally anticipated (of course, the reverse is also true, but counting on decreases in interest rates is risky). Finally, increasing an institution's debt can bring about a reduction in its credit rating—by such bodies as Moody's, for example—and such a reduction will be associated with a likely increase in the interest rates demanded for any future borrowing. These possible negatives are not a conclusive argument against institutions' using borrowing to cover short-term budgetary shortfalls, but they are a caution to do so sparingly, and, above all, not as a way to avoid needed strategic or operational changes.

D. Balancing Revenues and Expenditures

The Chronicle of Higher Education, in a particularly significant report, highlighted the unhappy choices facing public universities and colleges, due to the impact of the 2008–2009 economic crisis on state revenues, and consequently, on state support for those institutions. As state tax revenues dropped sharply, there was great pressure to decrease funding for higher education. One result was increases in tuition; or, as some legislators demanded, increased efficiency. Research budgets were squeezed. Deans insisted on a policy of minimum enrollments per class(usually associated with reductions in number of courses offered, and fewer multiple sections of those courses). Re-examination of curricula was stimulated. Demands were made, mostly from external sources, to extend on-line course offerings. There was even some thought given to increasing teaching loads for tenure-track faculty or—more likely—increasing the proportion of graduate students and adjunct faculty.[5]

The *Chronicle* report quoted the University of Arizona's (UA's) president, Robert N. Shelton, as stating that some legislators believe that higher education is a private, not a public, responsibility. In that context, the University of Arizona's goal is now to adapt to reductions in state aid by dumping degree programs that graduate too few students, and limiting programs to areas in which it thinks it can become a national leader. To those ends, UA's academic leaders plan to cut spending on administrative operations and increase overall revenue by ensuring that Arizona is competitive for research money in key areas. UA had almost $270 million worth of federally financed research in 2007, 10.5 percent less than in 2006. But, it still ranked 29th in 2007 among all universities in federal research money. Noteworthy is UA's firmly stated resolve that it would not increase on-line and distance learning, which it fears would dilute its emphasis on research. One major decision involved merging four of the university's colleges into a single College of Letters, Arts, and Science. Additionally, several low-enrollment degree programs in physics, secondary education, and the fine arts were considered for elimination.

A general conclusion, with profound implications, seems reasonable: public universities and colleges will become increasingly like their private counterparts, especially in reliance on tuition as a major source of revenue. They will also become more active in fund raising, as they seek to build endowments and enlarge research grants (perhaps with emphasis on research that promises to yield commercially valuable patents and royalties, in contrast to pure research). Other alternatives to reductions in state funding are difficult to envisage.

The economic crisis in 2008–2009 did not leave private academic institutions unscathed. Perhaps the most immediate, severe impact was on their endowments and the revenues they generated. The possible impact on enrollments and tuition revenues (especially when the increased pressure to raise unfunded financial aid is considered) will be better known by experience in the future. Generally speaking, they probably have greater flexibility to handle the current adversities than do their public counterparts, due, in part, to their greater discretion with regard to tuition increases, as well as their greater experience with fund raising from private sources. Those factors may provide them with a larger degree of diversity in prospective sources of revenue.

Efforts to achieve diversity of funding sources seek to minimize the external pressure on an academic institution. This makes vital the need for academic managers to engage in fund raising that will enhance the institution's endowments. With that thought in mind, it is also generally true—and should be no surprise—that trustees are expected to either make significant personal contributions, or to raise significant sums from others, or, indeed, to do both. Again speaking generally, there is a risk to the integrity of an institution from its reliance on trustees, or any other single substantial source of revenue. After all, the donors must understand that their efforts must have no "strings" attached. There must be no quid pro quo, no pressure to admit applicants who are unqualified or to grant special privileges in the form of otherwise unjustified financial aid or undeserved grades or even degrees. Needless to say, the pressure on the public university or college is from the legislature, and those institutions often employ professional lobbyists. Additionally, public universities and colleges often seek the help of legislators who reside within the political district where the university campus is located, because the institution is likely to be a major employer and economic factor in the local area's economy. Whatever the potential source of external pressure, the development of multiple sources of revenue contributes to the financial health of the university or college, and its ability to withstand unwelcome external pressures.

There is a caveat to the foregoing plea for larger endowments. Even a very large endowment, such as Harvard's, can't prevent the need for painful cutbacks in the event of a major downturn in economic activity, or of a ruinous inflation that destroys investments in debt securities. But, short of catastrophic developments, it is surely a decided benefit.

E. Mistakes to be Avoided

Budgets can be built top-down or bottom-up. The extreme example of the top-down type would be a budget constructed by the institution's president—perhaps with input from the board of trustees and his or her closest colleagues in the central administration—and presented to deans and other division heads to translate into detailed allocations to departments and other sub-units of the institution. Such a budget would be a dictate imposed from on high. Perhaps oddly, its greatest weakness, apart from its adverse impact on institutional morale, is that it would reflect mainly the aspirations, the abilities, and the financial comprehension of the president. It would be profoundly at odds with the tradition of faculty input into the governance of the university. It would probably have large negative consequences. Generally, top-down management budgets can be developed quickly, but they are executed slowly.

The extreme example of the bottom-up approach to budget building would be a budget aggregated from the aspirations of the faculty and the decision-making administrators of the non-academic units of the university. It would probably be only weakly—if at all—sensitive to the financial realities facing the institution as it moved up from departments to deans of schools and then to the president and the central administration. If some schools or colleges or departments were suffering low enrollments and consequent financial pressure, they would not likely press for their downsizing or elimination. More likely, they would argue that their cultural and intellectual importance to society warranted overlooking their financial weakness. Of course, their wishes would require redistribution of resources from other more "productive" departments. It does not require the intuitive insight of a seer to predict significant internal debate and confrontation. Clearly, some mix of the two budget-building approaches is desirable. To that end, university administrators are well advised to avoid the following mistakes.

Mistake 1: Failure to Invite Input from All Levels of Management

Academic leaders can achieve involvement of all levels of governance by uninhibited discussion of institutional aspirations and financial realities that involve the deans and the president (central administration). These meetings would be followed by meetings of the deans and their department chairs, followed by departmental meetings of the chairs with the tenure-track professors. Out of these meetings, a more realistic budget could be derived, which is informed about financial conditions. Such a budget, while it was aggregated from the departments up, would simultaneously be molded by further meetings between deans and chairs, and then by deans and the financial administrators of the central administration (on behalf of the president). But the final word could be reserved for determination in meetings between individual deans and the president. Such meetings stimulate involvement at all significant levels of administration, and, in turn, result in improved communications and reduce stress.

Mistake 2: Failure to Understand Budgeting Methodology and Practice

It is not necessary to take courses in accounting theory and practice to obtain an effective working understanding of financial statements and budgets, although having such training is certainly an asset. A metric device known as a dashboard can be useful in building budgets. The dashboard cascades the institution's mission and strategy throughout all levels of a university or college. It creates an interlocking system of objectives and indicators. The strength of the device is that it disseminates a clear understanding of every administrator's responsibility and accountability throughout the institution. Budgets built on such a base are superior to those imposed from above, or those aggregated from wish lists at lower levels of the university.

Notes

1. Paraphrased from Michael Shattock, *Managing Successful Universities*, 64–66.

2. Follow-up to John Sexton's memo titled: *Re-engineering II* (published June 1, 2009): 1–9, NYU copyright.

3. Ariel Kaminer, "Facing Criticism, N.Y.U. Will Cease Loans to Top Employees for Second Homes," *The New York Times*, August 15, 2013, A20.

4. *The Wall Street Journal*, May 29, 2009, C1.

5. *The Chronicle of Higher Education*, March 27, 2009, A1, A22–23.

Chapter 5

The Fundraising Challenge

A. Fundraising as a "Calling"

Presidents and deans must not feel personally rebuffed when they are refused by potential donors. They should see themselves as emissaries for a great "calling," one that offers a donor the opportunity to rise above material and personal considerations to accomplish a greater benefit for society—and perhaps achieve a modicum of immortality in the process. Professional fundraisers: (1) provide trained and experienced support staff who are equipped to organize the fundraising process; (2) help articulate objectives and priorities; (3) locate prospective donors and research their gift-giving capability and propensity; (4) arrange appropriate occasions for top administrators to offer gift proposals to prospects; (5) maintain follow-up communication so that momentum is not lost, and, when necessary, (6) encourage and educate the president and/ or the dean to "make the sale." Some administrators, recognizing the importance of the fundraising endeavor to the institution's financial ability to achieve its mission and strategy, enjoy the challenge that successful fundraising presents. Others, while recognizing its importance, are uncomfortable doing it; and, among these, are those who actively dislike the task, even find it demeaning to the dignity of the academic "calling." After all, there is nothing in the education of prospective professors (who are to be seekers and transmitters of knowledge) that prepares them for fundraising.

B. Fundraising as a Profession

Fundraising has become a substantial profession in America. The Mandel Center for Nonprofit Organizations at Case Western University in Cleveland, Ohio refers to the existence of over 200 programs designed to enhance "the effectiveness of nonprofit leaders and managers and the organizations they serve through education, research, and community service." The Center was established in 1984. Of course, effective fundraising is essential to the stated objectives. Case Western offers a graduate Master of Nonprofit Organizations (MNO) program, with two degree options. The option for students minus extensive professional experience consists of

> 60 credit hours of academic work taken over two years of full-time study, or approximately 48 months of part-time study. The program embraces a multidisciplinary curriculum consisting of four thematic areas: Nonprofit Purposes, Traditions, and Contexts; Analytic Thinking for Nonprofit Leaders; Generating and Managing Resources for Nonprofit Organizations (i.e., fundraising); and Leading Nonprofit Organizations." To cover these thematic areas, the program requires students to "take 33 credit hours of required courses and 17 credit hours of elective courses.

To satisfy the multidisciplinary needs of the program, the Mandel Center works with four sponsoring schools at Case Western: the College of Arts and Sciences, the School of Law, the Mandel School of Applied Social Sciences, and the Weatherhead School of Management.

The option for students with experience is designated as the Executive Option. It is "designed for nonprofit managers and practitioners with at least 10 years of professional experience and 5 years or more of management or supervisory experience." This option is a 45- credit hour program, comprising 30 credit hours of required courses and 15 of elective courses. The Executive Option usually requires 18 months of full-time study or about three years of part-time study. Students who register initially for the 60-credit hour program are not permitted subsequently to transfer into the 45-hour program. Presumably, this prohibition is designed to prevent possible gaming of the system.

New York University also has an established graduate program, which leads to a Master of Science in Fundraising degree. It is provided by the George H. Heyman, Jr. Center for Philanthropy and Fundraising, which is part of NYU's School of Continuing and Professional Studies. Established in 1999, the program has educated over three thousand practitioners, executives, and volunteers ranging in age from twenty to eighty. These students have come from many nonprofit, corporate, and foundation organizations. The inclusion of corporate organizations is appropriate, since many major American companies have established foundations and are significantly engaged in making research and other grants. The Center's mission statement notes, "Through a timely curriculum of scholarly and practical coursework, students explore the history, philosophy, and fundamentals of fundraising, the psychology behind giving, legal and ethical issues, and more." The program consists of eight required core courses, four elective courses, and a required capstone course involving a thesis research project. In addition, students in the program can avail themselves of internships and non-program courses offered by the School of Continuing and Professional Studies. The Heyman Center program is more sharply focused on fundraising than the one at Case Western. But both appear to be good examples of such programs, and they illustrate that fundraising has become an established profession. Finally, Advancement Resources, America's leading provider of research-based development training, held a Professional Fundraising Workshop for current and aspiring academic leaders, in August 2013, in Denver, Colorado.

C. Lobbying as a Profession

Lobbyists are paid intermediaries who have significant connections, usually to legislators and others in a position to direct grants and other funding by government agencies. They are employed also to affect governmental policies and legislation relative to regulation of business, and so on. Frequently, they are former legislators or government agency employees with experience in the inner working of legislative bodies and regulatory agencies. Significantly, *The Chronicle of Higher Education* reported: "Colleges and other educational entities spent more than $102 million in 2008 to lobby Congress and federal agencies, placing education seventh-highest on a list of industries ranked by the Center for Responsive Politics."[1] Almost the entire amount came from higher education, with a miniscule proportion coming from elementary and secondary educational institutions. In financial terms, the single largest spender was the State University of New York, which spent $1.6 million in 2008.

The aggregate amount of $102 million capped a ten-year trend in lobbying expenditures by higher education.

We have identified two universities in the Washington, DC area that offer courses in lobbying. They are Georgetown University and American University. Georgetown offers two courses: *Lobbying and Interests*, and *Shaping National Science Policy*. The former course examines the history of contemporary political lobbying, as well as conceptualizing the field and its impact on American politics. It considers the role of interest groups and their efforts to affect and direct government policy and action. It examines also the effects on political partisanship, the media, the technology of communication, and the possible corruption of the political system. The latter course focuses on lobbying efforts to shape America's science policy, an area with huge implications for our nation's future economic growth and well-being. Significantly, this course is cross-listed with that university's physics department (and 1 credit may be applied to the biology major).

American University offers six courses; namely, (1) The Art and Craft of Lobbying, (2) Workshop on Ethics and Lobbying, (3) European Public Affairs and Advocacy Institute (this course involves a work-study trip to Europe, with meetings with European experts in lobbying in Brussels, Berlin, Paris, and London), (4) Grassroots Lobbying, (5) Lobbying and the Internet, and (6) Political Parties, Interest Groups, and Lobbying. Once again, the professionalizing of the field seems apparent.

D. The Economic Environment and Fundraising

Despite the development and growth of fundraising as a profession, accompanied by expansion in the employment of its practitioners, we must recognize the inherent challenge that they face. Their success depends on their ability to convince those who have the financial capacity to make substantial contributions to actually part with a portion of their wealth. Apart from our urgent call to academic presidents and deans to be proactive in employing fundraising professionals to assist them, and to be active participants themselves in tailoring proposals to present to prospective donors and making the presentations, economic conditions are a major element in determining success or failure. When prosperity is prevalent and alumni and others feel flush, the task of the fundraisers is obviously easier. But when the reverse is the case, as it was in the severe economic recession of 2008–2009, then efforts must be intensified even if it only reduces the downturn in funds raised, rather than increasing or even maintaining them.

The essential point is that fundraising must be an ongoing and substantial effort in academic institutions. It does not take the place of other significant sources of revenue (tuition, research grants, and government), but it increases their diversity. Diversity of revenue sources is important because it can help moderate shortfalls from a particular source. Of course, when all sources suffer setbacks simultaneously, greater pressure is exerted on administrators to look harshly on expenditures and the efficiency of administrative procedures, as well as on academic policies such as majors and degree programs offered, mandatory class size minimums, teaching loads, maintenance and operation of plant (which can be starved for a short period, but invites a crisis if extended too long), financial aid packages, to mention some of the academic expenditure items (including those that are sacred cows of the Academy).

E. Fundraising Guidelines

The top administration of a university or college, as well as the development office, may find the following fundraising guidelines especially useful. They are listed in no particular order of importance.

1. Get the Board of Trustees "On-Board" with Fundraising Efforts

There is considerable misunderstanding of the role of the board of trustees in connection with fundraising. We discussed earlier the role of the board in the governance of the institution; in that respect, it is the final repository of institutional authority, and its most important decision is probably the hiring or termination of a president. Yet, while there is nothing in the formal and legal responsibilities of the board about fundraising, the reality is that its members do have such a responsibility. It is the most tangible evidence of their perception of the importance of the institution's mission. After all, why should others give, if the board is mute and miserly? There is a danger here, namely that an idea might spread that board memberships can be bought. The attitudes of the institution's president, as well as the board, are important in this connection. Perhaps the best protection against this perception lies in the criteria applied to prospective members; wealth should not be an overriding consideration. Prospective members should be people of substantial accomplishment, who command the respect of the community.

2. Make Special Efforts to Improve the Image of Your University in the Communities Where You Plan to Raise Funds

Communication is critical in this connection, but is insufficient by itself. There must be substance to be communicated, and such substance involves some soul-searching into the real goals of the institution, and how well those goals are being achieved. The accomplishments of alumni will speak for the university or college, as will the programs of study, the achievements and behavior of faculty and students, and the prominence of board members. With all that, the ability of the president and the deans to articulate mission and institutional contributions to the community at large will be critical.

3. Establish Clear and Targeted Fundraising Goals Directly Linked to the University's Strategic Plan

For example, the strategic objective of the University of Miami is to exhibit the characteristics of an A.A.U. university by 2015. One of the key steps in the strategic plan is to have an incoming freshman class with an average SAT score of 1300 by 2015. This objective is tracked through the indicator of average incoming freshman SAT scores by year. The indicator shows where the university currently stands, as well as the gap between the current year average and 1300. The size of the gap can be converted into the funds required for additional scholarships, to enroll new incoming freshman with SAT scores that will bring the average to 1300. This amount establishes a clear and targeted fundraising goal directly linked to the university's strategic plan.

4. Identify Critical Funding Sources for Each Goal

Some common sources are: (a) individual donors, (b) family foundations, (c) large corporate foundations, and (d) government agencies that provide research funds, as well as funds offering student loans and other direct subsidization of higher education. Susan C. Nelson, who assisted David W. Breneman and Chester E. Finn, Jr., reported that in the academic year 1974–75, a survey of 69 private universities showed that 50.3 percent of voluntary support came from individuals (26.6 percent from alumni and 23.7 percent from non-alumni), while 26.6 percent came from foundations, 14.9 percent from corporations, and 8.2 percent from other sources.[2] She also reported, in a much more inclusive examination of support for private higher education in academic year 1973–74, that private sources provided 64.3 percent of the total, while public sources provided 35.7 percent. The private sources broke down into 34.6 percent from unassisted tuition revenue, 11.4 percent from gifts, 6.4 percent from endowment, 8.0 percent from miscellaneous educational and general revenue, and 3.8 percent from student aid for tuition and fees. The public sources broke down into 21.7 percent from direct institutional support (18.0 percent from federal and 3.7 percent from state and local sources) and 10.0 percent from student aid for tuition and fees (8.3 percent from federal and 1.7 percent from state and local sources).[3]

a. Individual donors—The board of trustees, in addition to their personal gifts, should be a major source of leads, as well as active participants in making contacts and convincing prospects of the importance of supporting the institution. Individual schools and colleges may have their own boards of overseers that can be very helpful in fundraising campaigns. Such boards frequently exist within large universities.

b. Family foundations—A family foundation derives its funds from the members of a single family, at least initially. Subsequently, it may attract funds from other sources, based on the attractiveness of its mission. A famous recent case is the Melinda and William Gates Foundation, which, some years after its establishment by the Gates family, attracted a multibillion dollar gift from Warren Buffett, the renowned "Sage of Omaha." Usually, at least one family member serves as an officer or board member of the foundation, and, as donor, plays a significant role in governing and/or managing the foundation. Over the long-term, numbers of family foundations, especially large ones, move to management by nonfamily administrators. Well-known cases are the Ford and Carnegie Foundations. But, especially in smaller foundations, family influence, if not control, can last for several generations. Generally, participation by family members who serve as trustees or directors is on a voluntary basis, receiving no compensation. But there are cases where a family member is designated as the chief executive (e.g., executive director) of the foundation, and at a handsome salary. Family foundations, especially smaller ones, tend to concentrate their giving in areas that are related to problems that have afflicted a family member, or relate to some local community purpose.[4]

c. Large corporate foundations—A corporate foundation derives its grant-making funds primarily from the contributions of a profit-making business. The company-sponsored foundation often maintains close ties with the donor company but it is a legally separate organization, sometimes with its own endowment, and subject to the same rules and regulations as other private foundations.[5]

d. Government agencies—State governments are generally the major source of funding for public higher education institutions in their jurisdictions. At the top of the hierarchy are the research universities, of which there can be several in any of the more populous and wealthy states, e.g., California, New York, Texas, and Florida. Recently, as economic adversity diminished state revenues and legislatures wrestled with competing demands for funds, support for public higher education weakened. We have described elsewhere the actions taken by the state universities and colleges to offset reductions in state funding (raising tuition, especially on out-of-state students, and other actions). The point here is that public institutions need to re-examine the degree of their reliance on state funds.

5. Understand the Potential of Competitive Solicitations

With multiple fundraising activities common in large institutions, it is not unusual for situations to arise when the central administration (president and her or his development office) solicits the same prospective donors as does an individual school or college (dean and her or his development office). Some universities and colleges seek to avoid different units or individuals (e.g., central administration and deans) from soliciting the same donor source with competitive projects. They feel that failure to prevent competitive fundraising efforts will convey a negative impression of the efficiency of the asking institution, and may lose the prospective donor, while others hold the opposite point of view. They feel that competition is energizing, and yields larger results for the institution. We find no definitive proof of either viewpoint. In any case, ambitious, energetic deans and professors, as well as presidents are difficult to keep from soliciting donors where they have a contact that promises to get support for a desired research project, or an endowed chair, or endowed scholarships, or named facilities, and so on.

6. Recognize the Potential Pitfalls of Pledges

Academic fundraisers have a great temptation to include donor pledges in announcements of progress toward the achievement of campaign goals. The underlying idea is that they create an aura of progress that stimulates additional commitments, although one could argue that the impression of success could have the opposite outcome. Nonetheless, the common practice is to include pledges, as though they represent hard and binding commitments. Sometimes they actually do, being included in binding contractual documents or irrevocable provisions in wills. But they are often non-binding promises subject to later revocation. In that case, the gift is illusory, and the danger is that reliance on the promise can lead university leaders into expensive projects and financial commitments that become a burden on future budgets. When that happens, important academic programs and personnel may suffer, as "hard times" compel cutbacks and imperil the heart of the institutional mission.

Another potential pitfall involves donors who want to leverage their donations, i.e., demand that the university raise additional money from other sources to be added to their gift, thereby magnifying the impact of the original gift. Known as "matching gifts," they are fairly common, and usually involve a dollar-for-dollar match, doubling the size of the original grant. But there are cases where the original donor demands matches of several dollars for each dollar she or he has given. These donors usually expect full credit for the entire amount raised. We suggest wariness by president or dean when confronted by such a display of charitableness and magnanimity. Before accepting such matching gifts, make sure that every expectation of the donor is clear, explicit, and known, and that his or her commitment is legally binding (as evidenced by a formal contract or some equally firm document).

F. Tips for Approaching Individual Donors

Some useful tips as one prepares for an "asking":

1. Select Prospective Donors Carefully and Study Their Interests to Discover Possible Matches with University Objectives

It is very easy for an academic leader to become so fixated on a particular and favored objective, that she or he overlooks the attractiveness of that objective to a prospective donor. Enthusiasm in a president or dean is vital, but, in the vernacular, it "takes two to tango." What is critical is that there should be a match between the purpose of the proposed gift, and the interest of the donor. Consequently, pragmatism indicates that, before an "asking," adequate research should be directed to finding the purpose that will arouse the sympathy and generosity of the donor.

2. Seek Only Gifts that are Consistent with the School's Mission and Strategy

There is a great temptation to accept a gift, especially one that is substantial, even though the purpose of the donor is not consistent with the mission and strategy of the university or college. When approaching a donor, be sensitive to the interests of the donor. There is a hazard here that eagerness to announce a significant gift can lead an academic leader to undertake an institutional objective that is not truly consistent with the mission and strategy of the institution. The resulting strains and tensions can disrupt, misdirect, and weaken the institution. Perhaps the most relevant example would be the creation of an institute or center devoted to research and teaching in an area that is not compatible with existing institutional resources and the expertise of the faculty. But that is not to say that the interests of the donor should be ruling. When those interests are incompatible with the institution's mission and faculty strengths, the donor's dictate should not be accepted, and the donor's money should not sway the president or dean to accept it. The reason for the rejection need not become a basis for hard feelings. Our experience indicates that a careful explanation of the inherent conflict of purpose, coupled with sympathy for the donor's purpose in an appropriate institutional context, can obviate any ill-will.

3. Avoid Actions that Needlessly Aggravate or Alienate Important Fundraising Constituencies

Let us be completely clear: there must be no curbing by academic institutions of expression of ideas. After all, the touchstone in transmission and pursuit of knowledge is freedom of thought. Given that, we understand that this section may be construed by some as implying self-policing, perhaps to avoid alienating prospective donors. That conclusion would be a misinterpretation. An illustrative case of our concern involves Brandeis University, which attracted national press attention in early 2009. *The Wall Street Journal* reported the story, under the sensational headline "The Brandeis Bombshell."

> Without an apparent word of dissent, all 50 or so trustees approved a plan on January 26 to close the university's 48-year old Rose Art Museum and sell its entire 7,180 piece art collection; which was last appraised in 2006 at about $350 million. Brandeis's endowment had plunged to $540 million at the end of 2008 from $712 million as of June 30 of that year, and it was earning significantly less than the 8%-plus annual return on investment it had posted on June 30. Some of Brandeis's trustees are believed to have lost money from Bernard Madoff's Ponzi scheme, limiting their ability to make up the difference. . . . As the trustees looked ahead at the next four or five years, they could see operating deficits of $10 million to $20 million a year and little likelihood of Brandeis regaining its $700 million endowment and 8% interest income until 2015. The art collection looked like a big source of potential revenue. . . . The decision was heavily publicized and met with condemnation by museum and educational associations, as well as by individuals throughout the art world. . . . But current and future donors to Brandeis may hold a grudge, . . . if they believe that objects donated to the university will be quickly turned into cash.[6]

From a fundraising perspective, however, the major error involved communication—in particular, the failure to go beyond the administrative-trustee loop in arriving at so dramatic a decision. Of course, it is easy to be so prescient after the fact, but the lesson seems plain. Top administrators, trustees, and professional fundraising staff must be sensitive to the reactions, both internal and external, to the impact of decisions that involve turning donated assets into cash, to handle a financial emergency. A wider communicative and consultative process is needed than was true in the Brandeis case. The key point is that many, if not most, donors—especially those who make large donations—are usually "buying" a bit of immortality in memory of someone gone from the land of the living, or for their own memory. The notion that the donation might be used to meet a financial crisis could prove to be a powerful incentive to withhold future gifts, a consequence not to be ignored.

4. Accept Only Gifts Adequate for Their Purpose

The story of NYU's Center for Science and Technology Policy (CSTP) is instructive. It was transferred into the Graduate School of Business Administration (GBA) from the Graduate School of Public Administration (GPA) in 1981. It had been established in the GPA in 1978 and failed to achieve a viable relationship there. The factor that appears to have ruled the transfer from GPA to GBA was the enthusiasm of one person, the vice dean of GBA.

The prospective director of the CSTP appeared to be well connected in governmental and corporate scientific quarters, and seemed also to have credibility, fundraising ability, and managerial competence. At least that is how he appeared to the vice-dean, who perceived these additional advantages from the transfer of the Center to GBA: (1) it would bring a major source of funding for policy-oriented research on science and technology policy, economic growth, and international competitiveness; (2) the CSTP's research assistants were largely from GBA, and that relationship would be enhanced by a transfer from GPA; (3) the CSTP had a good support staff; (4) in GBA the Center would be a potential attraction for high-quality junior faculty having interest in the field; (5) the Center could serve as a focal point for raising GBA's emphasis on management in the technological environment of the future, and as a means for introducing executive programs and courses in those fields; and (6) the Center would encourage research in the study of energy and materials.

The vice dean perceived also some possible dangers: (1) a financial risk; (2) a diffusion of faculty interest and activity; (3) space problems (i.e., adequacy of physical plant); and (4) possible problems of allocation of overhead and other costs. Despite these potential problems, the vice dean was enthusiastic and pushed persistently in favor of moving the Center. The proposal was put before the faculty council. The chairman of the faculty council expressed concern that the transfer of the Center into GBA did not meet the criteria set down by the Council for the establishment of new Centers or Institutes. His objections focused on the criteria having to do with the match of purposes between Center and School, funding, and space requirements. Yet, a proposal to effect the transfer was put before the faculty council at its meeting on May 21, 1981, to be considered at the June 11 meeting. Since the council's chairman would be out of the country in June, he left the following memo as an expression of his views:

> In my view, the proposal does not meet the points stated in our criteria for institutes and centers, set down several weeks ago. The research focus of the Center is fuzzy, and, even when reasonably well articulated, the topics seem to be technical and far-removed from faculty expertise.
>
> • Faculty links (real and prospective) are superficial at best; people talk a good game, but when forced to specify precisely how the relationship is likely to evolve, the conversation often quickly evaporates.
> • The spillovers for our teaching programs are equally unclear, and any initiatives along these lines would necessarily have to come from the faculty if they are to succeed.
> • Aggressive fundraising by the Center is likely to cross lines with other funding priorities for GBA, no matter how hard we try to avoid this.
> • I am not convinced that the financial projections, in terms of real dollars, are at all realistic.
> • In short, I can think of some initiatives along these lines that would represent a worse "fit" for GBA than this one, but not many. I've said my piece, for what it's worth.

The rest of the story is quickly told. The Center was transferred in the absence of the council's chairperson, but the vice dean's enthusiasm was not fulfilled by ensuing events. The reality was that the council chairman's reservations proved correct. No true match of purposes existed between Center and School. Financing never fulfilled promises, so that deficits were experienced and financial strain was chronic. On July 2, 1986, the dean wrote to the director of the Institute that the Center had unfortunately not "become an economically viable enterprise nor has it garnered sufficient academic interest from our regular faculty." Consequently, the Center's relationship with GBA was terminated on September 1, 1986.

It took five years to terminate a Center that was brought into GBA against substantial opposition. Further, the opposition was clear, focused, and based on policies adopted by the faculty council. The lesson here is: be wary of narrowly based enthusiasm. A match of purposes and proper financing is needed.

Pleasant news is met as we turn from the Center for Science and Technology Policy (CSTP) to the Salomon Brothers Center for the Study of Financial Institutions, a leader among the Stern School's successful Institutes and Centers. Actually, that statement may be too restrained. The Salomon Brothers Center can make the claim that it is the foremost independent research organization for the study of problems and issues related to American and global financial structures. Its success clearly reflects the close match between the Center's purposes and those of its host school. Finance has long been a major area of strength in the Stern School. Its faculty has been in the forefront of important research output, and its curriculum and alumni have reflected the strength of which that productivity was indicative.

Equally important is the fact that the Salomon Brothers Center has attracted strong financial support. It began with a $3 million gift in 1971, of which $1 million was for space in Merrill Hall and $2 million for endowment (to be paid in annual installments over ten years). Further funding was received, e.g., endowment gifts to establish the Sidney Homer Directorship and the Charles Simon chair. Also, the Center receives operating funds from banks, securities firms, insurance companies, investment houses, and industrial companies in the United States. These contributors are called *Center Associates*.

Candor compels recognition of a delicate difficulty which sometimes comes up in sponsored research projects. Occasionally, the sponsor, who may be a business competitor of the firm that endowed the Center, balks at a research project supported by the Center that is prominently identified with another firm. The Center, while sometimes disappointed by such a reaction, has not yet suffered from a sponsor's desire to have its own purposes kept in view. The point to be made is that gifts by a named, active new center or institute can be frustrated if other and competitive entities hold back support because of the Center's name. The admonition remains relevant, although Salomon Brothers no longer exists.

Returning to its purpose, the Salomon Center focuses on: (1) supporting analyses of the dynamic, perhaps revolutionary, changes occurring in financial institutions and markets (especially important in the context of the national and international financial crisis that erupted in 2008); and (2) serving as an organizing and stimulating center for critical discussion of public policy issues surrounding the fast-paced evolution of financial systems.

To these ends, the Center does these things: (a) conducts academic research studies; (b) sponsors conferences that bring together academics, practitioners, regulators, and legislators; (c) publishes and disseminates working papers, monographs, and books on the results of the research and conferences; (d) presents leading-edge executive seminars in a "Frontiers of Finance" series; and (e) publishes, in cooperation with Basil Blackwell, of Oxford (England), two journals ("Financial Markets, Instruments, and Institutions." and the "Journal of International Financial Management and Accounting").

The match between the Center's purposes and those of the Stern School is enhanced and further illustrated by its "seed grants" and "Center Fellowships." The former uses that portion of the Center's funds reserved for grants to faculty, for pioneering research in financial and economic sectors, and for generating external funding. The latter applies Center funds to stimulate basic financial research at the Stern School by providing substantial, untied monies for the school's most productive middle-rank scholar/teachers and for visiting faculty members. The mutual strengthening of Center and School purposes, through this close interaction described, is enormously important. Such a match is necessary to the success of any institute or center.

5. Selecting Prospects

The selection of specific prospects (wealthy individuals) involves searching school records, seeking contacts and referrals from alumni and others who have already become donors and/or shown interest in the school, and studying press and other reports for alumni who have achieved prominence, but who have lost contact with the school. After a prospect is identified, his or her career, possible connections, interests, financial capacity, and record of charitable activity are studied. With that work done, a proposal is prepared that seeks to marry the donor's interest and the school's strategy and objectives. It is not enough that the dean, or one or more of the faculty, want a donor to give, thinking that their enthusiasm and purpose is reason enough for a gift. The donor needs to see why she or he should part with funds that could always be used in alternative ways. It is vital that the one seeking money perceive the interest and purpose of the prospective donor. To err here is to invite failure. When the donor's gift is tied to improper or tainted purposes, it is best not to consummate the proposal. There is no problem in providing a touch of immortality through a naming gift, or in showing appreciation by a reception, plaque, or painting marking the gift. But gifts that imply favoritism for an applicant for admission to the university, or a position as a trustee, are ill-advised and wrong. In some places such gifts are probably made and accepted. But such crassness only leads to the all-too-common perception that such practices are the norm at academic institutions. That perception helps destroy the good name of higher education nationally.

6. Set the Sights High

The behavioral insight behind this bit of advice assumes that prospective donors receiving proposals well below their ability and actual interest will think that the "asker" hasn't done his or her research, and doesn't appreciate the actual level of success achieved by the donor. While this may lead to a quicker affirmative response than might otherwise be the case, it can also result in a lesser success than was possible. It is assumed that donors are flattered to be seen as wealthier than might actually be the case, and, with some prospects, that possible reaction could lead them to stretch and do more than they otherwise might.

One episode made this principle vivid and unforgettable for the dean at NYU's School of Business. Early in his time in office, he sought alumni who had evidenced some interest in the School of Commerce, who had the financial ability to be significant donors, and who might also solicit and encourage others to give. A person soon appeared who met these specifications and had these characteristics. He was Mike S., an extraordinary man. Head of a successful accounting firm, he had achieved substantial financial success in real estate ventures and in rebuilding previously bankrupt businesses. He was a substantial contributor to many charities and was active among the School of Commerce alumni in fundraising activities.

The dean sought Mike S. and asked his help in raising money for the school. Mike was more than willing, and was of enormous importance over a period of years before he died. He raised millions of dollars for NYU and the School of Commerce. Mike was a natural fund raiser. He taught the dean many important lessons about fundraising. One of them was the difference between a "beggar" and a "real" fundraiser—one who got large sums of money. Mike explained, early in his relationship with the dean, that the most grievous error a fundraiser could make was to underestimate the ability or willingness of a prospect to donate. It was his firm belief that no prospective donor is ever insulted by being asked for a gift larger than he is able to give. He believed a donor, if solicited for too small an amount, would react partly with contempt for the fundraiser's ignorance and inadequate homework, and partly by giving less than what otherwise might have been given. The prospective donor would dismiss such a fundraiser as someone not to be taken seriously. Mike insisted that a person solicited for substantially more than he or she was able to give would be flattered. It was in that context that the episode of which we now speak occurred.

Associate Dean K, a long-service faculty member and administrator of the School of Commerce, retired. He was widely known and respected as an expert in writing and communication. He had authored popular texts on those subjects and done well financially as a result. Also a bachelor, with a penchant for sports cars, he was viewed as a sophisticated man about town. Some years after his retirement, word spread that he had married a much younger woman. The general reaction among his former faculty colleagues was that his money and sophistication had made him a "target," and he had succumbed to a woman who had her eyes on the former aspect. The then dean of Commerce had not known Associate Dean K. One day, to his surprise, he received a phone call from Dean K's wife, now a widow. She explained that K had left a will in which he provided funds for the school, and she wished to meet to discuss it. The dean agreed, and a time was set. Concurrently, the plans for Tisch Hall, to be the new home for the school, were well advanced, and the dean was busy raising money for that project. On that basis, he prepared some proposals to put to Mrs. K.

At the appointed time, Mrs. K appeared at the dean's office. A comely woman, perhaps in her late forties or early fifties, she quickly explained that Dean K had specified the purpose to which the money was to be put, and it had nothing to do with buildings. Somewhat disappointed, the dean concluded that the only thing left was to be courteous and invite the widow to lunch. On the way to the restaurant, Mrs. K asked the dean if he thought that program and related donations were more significant than those for buildings and other physical facilities. Thinking of Tisch

Hall, the dean replied that he was not in a good position to make such a distinction, because he was involved in a current project to build a new home for the school. Yet, he considered programs and improvement in student financial aid to also be vital concerns.

To his surprise, Mrs. K said that she agreed that buildings and other physical facilities were also important, as well as being attractive donor proposals. Having been conditioned by the conventional faculty opinion that Mrs. K married Dean K for his money, and having learned that in K's will he had made no financial provision for his widow—because she was otherwise well provided for—the dean began to propose naming-gift opportunities in Tisch Hall. Not knowing how well fixed the widow was, or her inclination to fund a naming gift for her late husband, the dean was diffident about the size of gift he proposed, beginning with a seat in an auditorium for $1,000. Through lunch, with no indication of any arousal of interest on Mrs. K's part, the dean gradually escalated the asking to $30,000, to name a classroom (these sums must be seen in the financial context of some four decades ago). Lunch was over, and the dean and Mrs. K were walking back to his office.

Suddenly, the dean realized that he was holding back on the size of his proposals, because of some preconceived notions about the widow. Also, he remembered Mike's advice. With that in mind, he remarked to Mrs. K that he had held back in his proposals. She asked: "Why?" He responded: "Because I have no idea of your financial status, and didn't want to seem brash and aggressive." She asked: "If you set aside those constraints, what would you propose?" The dean replied: "There is a major facility in Tisch Hall that will be used for important functions, and will provide an attractive place where faculty can relax and discuss school and other matters. It would be especially appropriate in memory of Dean K." Mrs. K asked: "What would it cost?" The dean said: "$100,000." The widow responded with the first show of enthusiasm, indicating that she wanted to make such a gift in memory of Dean K. In fact, she insisted that, upon their return to the office, her attorney should be called, and an agreement should be drawn. Within days, the dean received a check for $100.000. So much for the preconceived notions of the faculty. Finally, the dean gave mental kudos to old Mike for his wisdom. The dean realized that he had made a major mistake in his initial suggestions to Mrs. K.

7. Show Appreciation

An old adage states that the purest, and hence the noblest, charitable gifts are those made anonymously and without any hint of self-glorification. Some donors provide gifts of this kind and shun public disclosure of their generosity. But the overwhelming majority of donors welcome an indication of appreciation. Some are motivated to make their gifts because of the recognition and social status thereby obtained. It is a sound policy for a fund raiser to develop a pattern of recognizing significant gifts. Beyond simple expressions of gratitude, there are a number of customary, tangible means of evidencing appreciation, e.g., plaques, placed more or less prominently, depending on the magnitude of the gift; publicity about a gift in alumni or other publications; a reception; possibly a painting of the donor, displayed in an appropriate location, and so on. In connection with this principle, never surrender institutional and/or personal integrity. There should be absolutely no quid pro quo (such as the admission of unqualified students and the like) for donations.

Early in the 1968–1969 campaign to raise money for Tisch Hall at NYU, a "recognition" package was developed that became part of every proposal for a gift of $100,000 or more. (Today, the minimum amount would be significantly higher.) It included a wall plaque and/or listing on a lobby wall identifying patrons of the school, a reception recognizing the gift, an oil painting of the donor to be placed in an appropriate space, and a leather-bound album that contained photos of the reception and attendant ceremonies. If the donor did not wish any or all of these evidences of appreciation, they were dispensed with. But almost all enjoyed them, and the opportunity it afforded for friends and relatives to gather and congratulate the donor. Other expressions of appreciation accompanied gifts of lesser magnitude.

In the case of scholarships and fellowships, annual reports to donors are made telling them about the recipients and their accomplishments. Luncheons and receptions are also scheduled where donors and recipients meet. This arrangement is especially helpful in imparting a direct, one-to-one, personal contact that reinforces the donor's sense of having made an important gift. Also, it reinforces the donor's original motivation and often encourages follow-up gifts. It builds in the recipients a sense of gratitude and obligation that may well stimulate them to make gifts themselves in later years. In any case, annual reports to substantial donors are a good idea, even when gifts for purposes other than scholarships and fellowships are involved.

Notes

1. *The Chronicle of Higher Education*, February 13, 2009, A16.
2. David W. Breneman and Chester E. Finn, Jr., eds., *Public Policy and Private Higher Education*, (Washington, DC: The Brookings Institution, 1978), 132.
3. Ibid., 104.
4. Website of Illinois Donors Forum. This is a resource to guide philanthropic contributors to nonprofit institutions—in this case, in Illinois. It is also useful for institutions seeking such contributions.
        http://www.donorsforum.org/s_donorsforum/
5. Ibid.
6. *The Wall Street Journal*, February 3, 2009, D7.

Chapter 6

Other Aspects of Fundraising

A. Enhancing Revenues through Executive Education

Executive education programs can be profitable and generate surpluses. Beneficial results include supplemental compensation for full-time faculty, especially as support for research. Funds become available also for the use of qualified adjunct faculty In addition, these programs enable productive use of otherwise idle plant—a significant financial feature because there is almost zero marginal cost associated with that usage. Of course, a successful and expanding program would require investment in additional plant, but that would be a positive outcome that would enhance the other benefits.

Harvard University's Business School is an excellent illustration of the benefits just claimed. Its traditional MBA and doctoral programs are world famed. What is usually not realized is that its executive education and publishing operations far exceed, in revenues and staff, its traditional graduate academic degree programs. It is a simple observation of reality that these operations help support the academic programs, and the school's leadership does not hide that fact (as the 2009 annual report of the school makes plain). It needs to be understood that the support is much more than financial, because the executive education program provides raw material for faculty research and case development. Some data make the case more striking.

In 2009, the B school's revenue totaled $472 million. Tuition from executive education amounted to $107 million, and publishing revenue added another $137 million. In aggregate, these two revenue sources accounted for 51.7 percent of total revenue. If we add endowment distribution of $113 million, the three items account for 75.6 percent of total revenue. In sharp contrast, 2009 revenue from MBA tuition and fees amounted to $84 million, or 17.8 percent of total revenue. Clearly, executive education is an integral part of the mission of the school. With total 2009 expenditures of $438 million, operations yielded a surplus of $34 million. Looked at from another aspect, in 2009 the executive education program enrolled 9,345 students, compared with 1,809 MBA students and 120 doctoral students. The full-time faculty numbered 228, while the entire FTE (full-time equivalent) staff numbered 1,187.

A glance at the school's publishing operations is also instructive. At $137 million in 2009, they were the largest single source of school revenue (29 percent). In physical terms, they consisted of 8.3 million cases sold, 1.5 million books sold, a circulation of the Harvard Business Review amounting to 0.24 million, and 2.9 million reprints of HBR articles sold. But there is a danger lurking: academic leaders may be carried away by the lure of the revenue potential and overlook or, unhappily, compromise their dedication to the primary academic mission of their institutions. Awareness of the danger can prevent its occurrence.

B. Institutes and Centers as Fundraising Instruments

Presidents and deans are occasionally approached by faculty or some group or individual who indicate a willingness to make a substantial donation to establish a center or institute for research in some area of concern, with the avowed purpose of advancing knowledge in that area. There may also be another agenda and purpose, either explicitly stated, or implicitly understood: to promote some particular ideology, concept, or product. The sums dangled before the university administrator may be substantial enough to be very tempting, a figuratively alluring apple. Beware. Taking a bite can lead to a bad case of indigestion.

Our experience indicates that several factors are important in determining the success or failure of centers and institutes. They are: (1) a clear definition of purpose and mission; (2) funding adequate to the accomplishment of that purpose and mission; (3) support among the faculty, specifically a willingness to participate meaningfully in effecting the unit's mission and strategy; and (4) real external support in some business and/or government sector. All four of these conditions are necessary to the success of the center or institute. Other conditions are undoubtedly significant, e.g., the energy and competence of a director, but a deficiency in that area can be more easily overcome than a deficiency in one or more of the four critical factors.

Institute and center missions and strategies are variegated and can be fairly numerous. Some are more ambitious than others, seeking to achieve a wide spectrum of objectives. Others will be more limited in scope, satisfied with one or two objectives. Viewed broadly, institutes and centers may seek to do these sorts of things: (1) engage in research and publication of its results; (2) arrange conferences; (3) organize and operate management training programs; (4) support fellowships for graduate students; (5) support an endowed professorship—typically for the unit's director; (6) engage in fundraising to further the work of the unit; (7) educate future teachers to advance the mission of the institute/center; and (8) act as a recruitment intermediary in behalf of an industry or some other external entity.

The foregoing activities do not address the critical and central matter of mission or strategy, i.e., the end for which these things are means. The end must be clearly defined. A multitude of activities unaccompanied by a clear definition of mission and strategy is likely to fail to generate the internal and external support necessary to success. Typically, statements of purpose involve focusing on performing the objectives noted in behalf of an *industry, government sector, or cause.* The first two are more self-evident than the last. For example, an 'Institute for Retail Management' or a 'Center for Urban Planning.' An example of the last named purpose would be an 'Institute for Entrepreneurship,' or an 'Institute for the Study of Quality in Manufacturing and Service.'

In some cases, institutes and centers can be created without approval from the central administration and board of trustees. In other cases, the central administration and the board of trustees must approve all institutes and centers. In the first case, institutes and centers are easily created. In the second case, there is greater difficulty. The reason is evident: once created, they bring into place people who have a vested interest in their perpetuation, let alone their expansion. In this regard, at least two dangers face presidents and deans. First, there are almost always individuals among the faculty and/or external to it who will promote a new institute or center; second, if some funding is available, then the temptation to go ahead can be powerful.

But the funding may be inadequate, and therein resides the danger; for the immediate prestige of being able to announce a gift that seems significant on its face is most enticing. The point is: don't be hasty to seize a dollar offered now, when it entails getting four or five more to accomplish the intended mission. Although institutes and centers may be easily created, they cannot be so easily destroyed. Centers and institutes, once created, generate emotional and vested interests within the school or college in which they reside. Their termination may involve termination or reassignment of faculty and/or administrators. There is also the reaction of donors to the center or institute, as well as external public and/or private groups and individuals with strong opinions about the value of the affected center or institute, an evaluation that may not be shared by the university's or college's faculty and administration.

C. Creating Other Resources to Support the Academic Mission

In addition to creating financial resources to support research, research that has marketable outcomes inspires licensing arrangements that produce income. Table 6-1 shows data for 25 universities that produced the most licensing income in fiscal 2009. It indicates also the number of new start-up companies they created and the number of new patent applications they submitted to the federal government for approval. It does not, however, show the number of universities in each category of licensing revenue. None the less, it is a significant activity, and an area that warrants attention by academic institutions.[1]

Table 6-1

25 Universities with Most Licensing Revenue (fiscal 2009)

Licensing Revenue	Startup Companies Created	New Patent Applications
$150 million and Over	16	370
$100 million to $150 million	52	978
$50 million to $100 million	8	1,334
$25 million to $50 million	6	899
Under $25 million	7	845

Perhaps the most striking example of the point being made here is provided by the University of Florida at Gainesville, known in the sports world as the "Gators." UF is Florida's leading public research university, respected nationally as an academic institution. It is also one of the nation's top Division I sports centers, known especially as a football power, and a leading member of the Southeast Conference. Some years ago, in an effort to overcome the fatigue accompanying strenuous, highly competitive athletic exertion, its research labs developed an energy drink which was appropriately called Gatorade. The rest is history. Knowledge of the benefits of Gatorade spread quickly and widely; followed by a huge demand for the magic liquid. UF arranged for its commercial production and distribution, which produced a substantial revenue stream for the university. Eventually, the patent was sold for hundreds of millions of dollars. In short, marketable outcomes of university research labs are no penny ante matter. They are also attractive targets for computer hackers world-wide, who break into their computer systems seeking to steal and sell valuable research discoveries (more on this in chapter VII). There is more to this story. Licensing income embraces Division I sports revenue from licensing permission to producers of sports clothing, shoes, memorabilia, equipment, etc., to use a university's logo on these items. A "pretty penny" is received in return.

D. Fundraising as a Source of Leadership Power

In the self-governing structure of American higher education, presidents usually deal directly with deans, who are seen by the faculty as their agents to central administration and to the outside world. Presidents and deans are primarily academicians, not industrial managers or executives. Although they are clearly possessed of a managerial role, their role as academic leaders is dominant. In this context, a president who achieves substantial success as a fund raiser is empowered in relations with her/his board of trustees and deans, while a dean enjoying fund-raising success is empowered in relations with both his/her faculty and the central administration (including the president).

This is not a case where power grows out of the barrel of a gun. Instead it derives from financial strength. In the case of the president, additional funds make possible new initiatives that will enhance the prestige of the university, as well as buttress established areas of excellence. On the faculty side, it is the ability of a dean to break budgetary bonds and use discretion in supporting various school initiatives. Faculty can be attracted to follow directions they otherwise might not, whether in programs, research, or teaching. And central administration is less likely to inhibit such initiatives. Further, an aura of success surrounds such a dean's school, and that aura lends status. Entrepreneurship and innovation are rewarded in the academic world, as well as outside it.

E. Fundraising from Public Sources

Public universities and colleges rely heavily government funding, and we have written about the difficulties associated with that reliance. For example, we referred to the current problems of the University of Arizona, as well as the University of California and other public institutions. Almost all of them are feeling severe financial pressure because state legislatures are wrestling with substantial revenue shortfalls. In addition, they are simultaneously being confronted with serious but competing needs of important programs other than higher education. From 2008 to 2013, state appropriations to higher education declined in 48 of the 50 states; the degree of decline ranging from a relatively modest -5.1 percent to a huge -42 percent in Arizona. They increased in only two states; by 11.9 percent in Alaska, and by 21 percent in Wyoming.[2] The decline is moderated somewhat if we include federal support. The data for 2010–2011 shows decreased support in 33 states and *increased* support in 17 states.[3]

The financial problem is not limited to the public institutions. Private universities and colleges, while more dependent on tuition revenues and income from endowments and gifts as well as research, have also become reliant, to a significant degree, on both federal and state funds for scholarship support, research grants, and direct subsidies. Of course, there is a resultant tension here between the public and the private institutions, but it is not new. In a prescient study published in 1978, the Brookings Institution focused on this issue.

> Despite the manifest complexity of the issues, the authors conclude with two straightforward propositions. First, anyone seeking to solve the dilemmas facing private higher education in the 1980s cannot avoid a fundamental policy choice between making private colleges financially more like public ones, or public colleges more like private ones. Second, federal and state education policies have to be consciously

coordinated (as they rarely have been in the past) if a strong and balanced system of higher education is to be preserved.[4]

The climate favored following the public model when the foregoing was written, more than three decades ago. But times have changed, and now the reverse appears a more likely outcome; that is the thrust of an article published in *The Chronicle of Higher Education*.[5] The article observed that some academicians, as well as legislators, were seeking to reduce the reliance of public institutions on state funds. Of course that means increased reliance on tuition, research grants, and private donations, as well as attention to greater operational efficiency. All the while, there needs to be continued emphasis on the improvement, let alone the preservation, of quality in teaching and research. The article noted that a number of public universities, like the University of Michigan, have developed diverse revenue sources that make them seem more akin to private institutions than to the traditional public institutions. But the majority of public universities and colleges continue to depend on their state legislatures. The picture seems clear: public institutions are under pressure to develop non-governmental sources of revenue (most likely tuition increases, endowments and gifts, and research grants). In the meantime, they are unlikely to sever their ties to their respective states, even though they will move toward the Michigan paradigm.

Organizationally, the relationships with the several layers of government that provide financial and other forms of support could follow the example of the University of Oregon, or some variant. The University of Oregon's Office of Government Affairs handles relationships with federal, state, and local governments. It insures that the university's interactions with governmental agencies and its stakeholder communities are healthy, well informed, and mutually beneficial. Larger universities and colleges have important interaction with local, regional, national, and international governmental entities. Smaller institutions do not have so extensive a reach, but are still involved with several levels of government. An 'Office of Government Affairs' can promote mutual understanding and those supportive relationships necessary for healthy collaboration with federal, state, and local governments, and with various community members. At the University of Oregon, an Office of Federal Affairs[6] coordinates the activities of the university on matters relating to the federal government and Congress. Staff members develop and implement the university's federal agenda; monitor federal legislation, programs, and proposals; assess potential implications and opportunities; and serve as liaison between the university and members of the state congressional delegation, congressional committees, and federal agencies. The university's Office of State Affairs coordinates the activities of the university on matters relating to its state financial support and legislative priorities. Staff members serve as the liaison to the state's board of higher education and its legislature, monitoring legislative and policy initiatives. They also manage the university's advocacy program and provide staff for legislative committees of the board of trustees and alumni association board of directors.

F. Endowments in Public and Private Universities and Colleges: Some Implications

The AAUP's 2008–2009 economic report on the status of the profession noted a significant difference between the importance of endowments in public and in private universities and colleges.

Analyzing ten public and ten private universities with the largest endowment value per fulltime equivalent student—and the relationship between that figure and the average contribution of endowment and gifts to operating budgets—the report found: (1) the average endowment per FTE student at the public universities was, in round numbers, $124 thousand, while at the private universities it was $1.3 million; and (2) the average contribution of endowment and gifts to the operating budget at the public universities was 8.9 percent, while at the private universities it was 40.5 percent. This is a striking difference, and helps explain fundraising pressure, especially at private institutions. It seems reasonable to expect that, as substantial revenue shortfalls spread in the states, which then move to reduce their support for their respective public universities and colleges, the pressure in those institutions to increase other revenue sources will intensify. One move will be to increase tuition charges, especially for out-of-state students, while another will be to seek an increase in gifts and endowments. Of course, there also is the expenditure side of the picture. Pressure is likely to grow, especially among the public institutions, to increase operational efficiency and productivity. That pressure is likely to be associated with demands for expansion in on-line learning, with significant implications for traditional modes of teaching and learning.

Looked at in fiscal year 2010, there were 217 colleges and universities with endowments of $250 million and more. Of that number, 62 had endowments of $1 billion and more; 66 had endowments of $500 million to $1 billion; and 89 reported endowments of $250 million to $500 million. Of those with endowments of $1 billion and more, 18 were public institutions and 44 were private not-for-profit. Twelve were Ivy League schools (Harvard, Yale, Princeton, Columbia, etc.)[7]

G. The Role of Endowments: A Challenge in Budgetary Policy

Endowments play a substantial budgetary role that affects the well-being and success of academic institutions in achieving their institutional goals. But academic leaders face a challenge in this area of their responsibilities, a challenge consisting of the complexity of investing decisions, coupled with the competitive claims of multiple would-be recipients of funds that collectively can exhaust the ability of an endowment to serve as a budgetary cushion in periods of financial adversity. Let us consider the wealthiest universities—Harvard and Yale.

Plainly, if Harvard did not have a very large endowment, it simply could not sustain its renowned position as the leading research university. It must be kept in mind that Harvard's endowment, which peaked in early 2008 at just below $37 billion, suffered sharp losses of some $8 billion by the end of that year, with no guarantee against further significant losses as the financial crisis of 2008 continued into 2009 when an additional loss of some $3 billion occurred. In addition to critics who complained that Harvard did not expense its endowment as freely as it should, there were other critics who were unhappy because the managers of Harvard's endowment followed investment policies that were insufficiently sensitive to social and political considerations, e.g., investments in firms operating in countries with dictatorial regimes and/or firms that allegedly exploited labor and/or lacked concern with environmental issues. Of course, these concerns overlooked the fiduciary obligation of the managers to manage the endowment with financial prudence.

David Swensen, Yale's chief investment officer, was a pioneer in turning the university's investment policy in new directions, i.e., from primary reliance on stocks and bonds to newer investment instruments such as hedge funds, private equities, and oil and gas. According to an interview reported by *The Wall Street Journal*, that reorientation yielded a 16 percent average annual return in the 1998-2008 decade (through June 2008), as compared with a 2 percent average annual return for the Standard &Poor's 500-stock index. During that decade, Yale's endowment (assets) tripled to $23 billion, exceeded only by Harvard's peak of $36.9 billion. This sterling record was based on a riskier investment policy, which became clear later, in the financial crisis of late 2008, when the endowment lost one-fourth of its value (almost $6 billion), concurrent with Harvard's endowment loss of some $11 billion. But this change of fortune did not faze Mr. Swensen, who pointed out that his policy was truly long-term, and unaltered by essentially shorter-term fluctuations in the financial markets. He added a significant qualification by observing that simply investing in hedge funds, for example, or, more importantly, in funds of funds, with the idea that large returns would therefore ensue, was blind and doomed to failure. Yale did not hire others to manage their investments. Instead, Yale had its own team of investment analysts and experts (20–25 in number) who studied and obtained intimate knowledge of any funds or other entities that it chose to invest in. Doing this, Yale believed, would guarantee independence of investment judgments, and avoid or minimize any fee payments to other investment managers.

While universities should seek the development of substantial endowments, an over reliance on endowment income and annual expensing from corpus can become a trap. A sudden and drastic decline in financial markets such as occurred in 2008, with great uncertainty as to any recovery of those losses, wreaks havoc on both corpus and income as major sources of budget support. While Yale and Harvard have large endowment cushions, they are not immune to large losses in corpus. With endowment and investment income providing almost 38 percent of Harvard's revenue, spending decisions required closer control than might otherwise have been the case.

A report in *The New York Times* noted that Harvard, while wealthy, was short on cash.[8] It relied on its endowment to provide more than a third of the money for its operations. Yet, the endowment was on course to post its biggest loss in forty years. Much of its money was tied up for the long term, so the university had to struggle to meet some obligations. Harvard froze salaries for faculty and nonunion staff members, and offered early retirement to 1,600 employees. Harvard Divinity School warned it might not be able to cover tuition for all its students with need, the School of Arts and Sciences cut its billion dollar budget by roughly

10 percent, and the university president announced that the unprecedented drop in the endowment was causing it to delay its planned expansion into the Allston neighborhood of Boston with a $1 billion Science Center. The university, as we noted earlier, added to its debt by issuing $1.5 billion in new bonds to meet current cash needs, its largest such offering ever.

Yale's endowment was off 13.4 percent, while Princeton's was down 11 percent in a comparable four-month period, and both projected a total 25 percent drop for the fiscal year. But Harvard's experience was magnified by its use of leverage in its investment policy. This multiplied the amplitude of variation up and down from what would have resulted, if a more conservative approach had been followed. In this connection, *The New York Times* report stated:

> The endowment was squeezed partly because it had invested more than its assets, a leveraging strategy that can magnify results, both good and bad. It also had invested heavily in private equity and related deals, which not only lock up existing cash but require investors to put up more capital over time.

There is danger in large dependence on endowments as a major source of revenue for sustaining ongoing institutional expenditures. We do not advocate hoarding of endowment funds, but we do suggest that they should be treated as a substantial cushion, which can moderate the effects of sudden changes in other revenue streams, i.e., tuition, grants for research, income from patents gained from research with marketable applications, government funding, and so on. So treated, endowments can act as a contra-cyclical financial instrument. But this requires care and prudence in investments, and avoidance of using endowments as instruments of social or political reform. *The New York Times* report cited spokesmen for Cornell, Syracuse, and Dartmouth, who forecast a dire budgetary picture in the coming months (2008–2009), and possibly years, with stringent cutbacks in plans and operations. The cushioning role potential of endowments is clear in these cases.

We cannot leave the discussion of endowments without commenting on the rationale that led David Swensen of Yale, and others responsible for investment decisions, to shift from the long-accepted conservative tradition—a portfolio of stocks and bonds—to hedge funds, private equity operators, real estate, and other investments that offered current higher returns, but turned out to be high risk. A joint report of endowments by *The Chronicle of Higher Education* and *The Chronicle of Philanthropy,* published some three years before the economic collapse of 2008–2009, offers a lucid and compelling explanation:

> Nonprofit endowment managers expect that, over the next decade, what was once a standard portfolio composition, 60 percent in stocks and 40 percent in bonds, will produce returns of just 6 percent to 8 percent annually. If inflation increases at 2 percent to 3 percent, as it did in prior years, such returns may not be enough to preserve the purchasing power of an endowment that spends 5 percent of its assets each year. [That was the widely-accepted standard used by research universities and other nonprofit institutions.] So endowment managers are taking a variety of approaches . . . But the most popular strategy is to increase exposure to alternative investments, including private equities (such as venture-capital funds and 'buyout' funds, which look to take over existing companies and improve their returns), timber, oil and gas, and, especially, hedge funds. Ten percent of the assets in the 210 endowments . . . [surveyed] . . . were invested in hedge funds. An annual survey of 317 foundations and operating charities by the Common Fund Institute . . . which manages $34 billion for nonprofit institutions, found that the proportion of endowment assets committed to hedge funds increased by 50 percent (from 6 percent to 9 percent) from 2003 to 2004.[9]

Viewed retrospectively some ten years later, it is clear that one must become wary of jumping in and following the lead of the most sophisticated, the most aggressive, and often the blindest guides in their understanding of risk.

We would be remiss if we failed to describe Columbia University's endowment policy. It has an endowment that was valued at $7.1 billion as of June 30, 2008, although it was diminished by 22 percent as of March 2009 (about $1.6 billion, to about $5.5 billion).[10] But where Harvard relied on its endowment to cover some 38 percent of its operating budget, and Princeton relied on its endowment of some $16.2 billion to provide 45 percent of its operating budget, Columbia relied on its endowment to cover only about 13 percent of its operating budget. Also, Columbia did not leverage its endowment, in an effort to swell returns despite increased risk. Further, Columbia's fundraising in 2009 was very successful, bringing in a record $495 million. Its research grants also have held up well. Concurrently, Columbia's $4 billion capital campaign is ahead of schedule, having brought in a little less than $3.2 billion so far. We can narrow the focus somewhat: 13 percent of Columbia's $3 billion operating budget amounts to $390 million. If we assume that the endowment was yielding a 6 percent return, then a $7.1 billion endowment would produce some $426 million, and when diminished to $5.5 billion it would produce some $330 million. Compare these sums with the $390 million estimated as the actual experience of the current operating budget, and it appears that, assuming no decrease in the operating budget, the shortfall is some $60 million. That is a relatively manageable problem with a $3 billion budget. In fact, unlike Harvard and some other leading universities, Columbia has not had to issue bonds to meet cash-flow needs. In fact, Columbia adopted an operating budget for the 2009–2010 fiscal year that was actually $12 million greater than the current year's budget. The amount is miniscule, but compared with the crisis situation in so many other prestigious universities, Columbia's experience is worth noting.

Of course, Columbia is not free of all financial pressure. The budgetary balance is subject to pressure should economic conditions deteriorate further, but Columbia is able to take a more measured approach than others by virtue of its financial policies. For one thing, its credit rating has not been reduced from AAA. The university is one of the twenty private and public colleges and universities out of 530 institutions to which Moody's Investment Service gives the highest rating. Beyond that, Columbia has taken these steps: (1) selective layoffs of management and administrative positions, coupled with a slowdown, but not a freeze, on hiring; (2) notifying the university's schools and centers to figure on a decline of 8 percent in next year's endowment income when they prepare their individual budgets; and (3) varying with the individual school's analysis, an increase in admissions (Columbia College, for example, plans to increase its new freshmen class by fifty students). Perhaps the modest size of Columbia's endowment compared with Harvard, Yale, or Princeton was a blessing in disguise, because it limited the degree of reliance on it as a major source of operating revenue. But that conclusion fails to give credit where credit is due because Columbia could have followed riskier investment policies, even leveraging, to swell income. But it did not do so, and in its experience we believe there are some lessons.

Perhaps most important, the endowment should be viewed as a contra-cyclical element in the budget. That means that in prosperous times the endowment should be built up through strong fundraising, prudent, but some, increased risk (perhaps 15 to 20 percent of the corpus) in alternative investments, avoidance of any leveraging in investments to swell earnings (don't get greedy), coupled with prudent expenditure policies. Unfortunately, reality does not parallel our proposed contra-cyclical policy recommendation. Jeffrey R. Brown, Stephen G. Dimmock, Jun-Koo Kang, and Scott J. Weisbenner reported the actual behavior of university and college presidents in the March 2014 issue of *The American Economic Review* ("How University Endowments Respond to Financial Market Shocks: Evidence and Implications"). Their research revealed that in rising markets, university leaders seek to build their endowments (save). But, in declining markets, they quickly cut endowment payouts. They term this "The Endowment Hoarding Hypothesis." They suggest that this behavior reflects presidential belief that personal compensation and prestige, as well as institutional prestige, are all enhanced by the size of the endowment.

Expenditure policies are an integral element in endowment management, because, especially during prosperity, there will be many claimants seeking to invade the endowment for their always (self-perceived) "socially" beneficial purposes. Faculty will want better compensation and benefits, more money dedicated to their particular areas of research interest, more and better housing, possibly reduced teaching loads, as well as other items. Students will resist increases in tuition, press for greater financial aid, want more and better housing and recreational facilities, desire more full-time faculty teaching classes, plus other amenities that their fertile minds will discover. Of perhaps even greater immediate significance for endowments, there will be 'politically correct' people who clamor that some of the endowment should be invested with an eye to social, political, and economic policy objectives dear to their hearts, even though such investing may be costly to the endowment's future usefulness as a budgetary cushion. Presidents must keep these factors in mind, decide what uses they wish to promote with the endowment, articulate those goals clearly, and then implement them.

Endowments are built from gifts from individuals, foundations, companies, and others, and are usually associated with active, professional campaigns. These campaigns have become a ubiquitous aspect of research universities. A significant element is a desire to raise money that is unrestricted, and available for use to help defray current expenses. Even in the negative period of 2008–2009, annual giving was substantial, though reduced from the prior year. Of 74 private research universities detailed in the annual Council for Aid to Education's *Voluntary Support of Education* report, a total of $8.4 billion was received, while 144 public research universities reported receiving $9.4 billion. Interestingly, of these sums only 15.3 percent was contributed by the alumni of the private institutions, and 9.6 percent by the alumni of the public institutions. It appears that the alumni bodies represent a fund-raising challenge. Although the aggregate dollar sums cited appear large, they were significantly smaller than in the prior year; being down by 9.7 percent in the private universities and 13.2 in the public. If we look at fiscal year 2010, however, and, look at overall endowments, the picture is dramatically different. In public universities, they grew by 12.0 percent, and in private, non-profit institutions they grew by 11.8 percent.[11]

A particularly interesting arrangement was reported by Cornell University. It involved a discount offered to Sanford I. Weill, a major donor and emeritus trustee who had made a $250 million pledge, to be given over a period of time. Cornell offered Mr. Weill a discount on the pledge if he agreed to pay the discounted sum immediately. Following negotiations as to the current value of the pledge, an agreement was reached, and Mr. Weill and his wife made cash gifts of $170 million. Cornell also reported another interesting arrangement made possible by the existence of its loyal donor base. The university suggested to these donors that, instead of making major endowment gifts, they make cash gifts equal to what their intended donations would have paid out from the endowment in that year. Almost 200 donors agreed to the plan, thereby easing Cornell's financial situation in 2009. These illustrations indicate how intelligent fundraising can work in an adverse financial environment.

H. A Comparative Analysis

We selected three private and three public universities for a comparative financial examination, but not randomly. See Tables 6-2 and 6-3. We understand that it is dangerous to deduce too broadly from so limited a selection, but we hoped that, within the confines of our limited investigative resources, we might gain some preliminary insights. Our choices were guided partly by our familiarity with three of the schools selected (NYU, U. of Miami, and Montclair State—a regional university). Harvard was included because no consideration of American research universities can proceed without examination of the nation's wealthiest and probably best known institution. Harvard, Miami, and NYU are all private research universities, but at different stages of development, although all three are recognized as major research institutions. Harvard has been a leader for generations.

NYU is newly arrived among the nation's top research institutions, while Miami is making rapid progress into the top ranks. Of the public universities, Florida and Alabama–Tuscaloosa were selected because of their prominence in Division I sports, accompanied by their large differences as research institutions. Montclair State is an outlier. It is a teaching institution with master's programs, and, in the business school, a strong desire to move up academically in the research area. It seemed to offer an interesting comparative backdrop for the other institutions. We note also that the financial data are not for the same academic year, varying between 2005 and 2008. Despite differences in the original classification of the several revenue and expenditure categories, we tried to fit all the institutions into a uniform classification model.

We observe: (1) student fees and tuition revenues are of major importance in all institutions (both private and public), except Florida, where it represented 8.9 percent of total revenue, while government aid amounted to 42.9 percent of the total; (2) although student fees and tuition accounted for 20.5 percent of total revenue at Harvard, that figure includes income from the business school's executive education program (which outweighs that institution's traditional academic programs in numbers of students and dollars) and income from Harvard's Extension School; (3) NYU's heavy reliance on income from students (50.2 percent) reflects its history, and recent arrival in the top echelon of research institutions, which tend to be more heavily endowed on a per student basis; (4) while NYU has achieved the aura of a top research university, sponsored research amounted only to 13.5 percent of total revenue, as contrasted with Miami's 42.6 percent and Harvard's 20 percent (of course, the percent figures are affected by the numerical base underlying their computation), i.e., Harvard's 20 percent represents $642 million of sponsored research, and Miami's 42.6 percent represents $463 million of sponsored research (we think Miami's figures include the medical center); (5) turning momentarily to expenditures, an anomaly appears (Miami's spending on research represents only 17 percent of total expenditures or $195 million, while NYU's spending represents $275 million or 12.8 percent); (6) investment income dominates Harvard's revenue picture (37.6 percent of the total), but is small at the other institutions

Table 6-2

Revenues and Expenditures of Private Universities

Revenues	Harvard University $(000)	% of total	NYU $(000)	% of total	University of Miami $(000)	% of total
Student Income	657,627	20.5	1,077,675	50.2	357,000	33.0
Sponsored Research	641,934	20.0	290,036	13.5	462,600	42.6
Gifts for Current Gifts	253,994	6.7	87,697	4.1	85,900	8.0
Investment Income	1,208,278	37.6	112,421	5.2	66,000	2.9
Auxiliary Services			331,995	2.2	92,300	2.2
Other	488,573	15.2	246,813	11.2	30,400	11.3
Total Revenues	**3,210,506**	**100.0**	**2,146,637**	**99.7**	**1,094,200**	**100.0**

Expenses	Harvard University $(000)	% of total	NYU $(000)	% of total	University of Miami $(000)	% of total
Instruction	683,010	27.8	1,116,305	52.2	413,700	35.9
Research	559,314	17.6	273,059	12.8	194,800	17.0
Libraries	197,939	6.2	57,182	2.4	0	0.0
Academic Support	570,068	17.9	96,727	4.5	173,800	15.0
Institutional Support	562,255	17.7	228,206	10.7	239,500	20.8
Auxiliary Support	398,064	12.6	367,654	17.2	129,800	11.3
Total Expenses	**2,970,650**	**99.8**	**2,139,113**	**99.8**	**1,151,600**	**100.0**

Table 6-3

Revenues and Expenditures of Public Universities

Revenues	Montclair State University		University of Florida		University of Alabama (Tuscaloosa)	
	$(000)	% of Total	$(000)	% of Total	$(000)	% of Total
Student Income	133,492	47.9	167,600	8.9	135,420	24.2
Sponsored Research	388	0.1	695,200	37.0	65,092	11.6
Gifts for Current Use	0.00	0.00	00.00	0.0	42,323	7.5
Investment Income	5,943	2.1	29,100	1.5	46,192	8.2
Auxiliary Services	56,118	20.1	178,600	9.5	114,177	20.4
Government Aid	79,147	28.4	808,500	42.9	145,932	26.0
Other	3,886	1.4	2,100	0.2	11,463	2.0
Total Revenues	**278,974**	**100.0**	**1,881,100**	**100.0**	**560,599**	**99.9**

Expenses	Montclair State University		University of Florida		University of Alabama (Tuscaloosa)	
	$(000)	% of Total	$(000)	% of Total	$(000)	% of Total
Instruction	84,592	33.8	548,500	30.3	143,505	28.9
Research	811	0.3	460,600	25.4	26,079	5.3
Libraries	44,238	17.7	200,600	11.1	75,477	15.2
Academic Support	68,787	27.5	363,000	20.1	118,686	23.8
Institutional Support	40,243	16.1	130,000	7.2	83,753	16.9
Auxiliary Support	11,378	4.6	108,500	6.0	48,763	9.8
Total Expenses	**250,019**	**100.0**	**1,811,200**	**100.1**	**496,114**	**99.9**

(5.2 percent at NYU, 2.4 percent at Miami, 1.5 percent at Florida, 8.2 percent at Alabama–Tuscaloosa, and 2.1 percent at Montclair State); (7) the relatively, higher percentage at Alabama–Tuscaloosa probably includes funds restricted to support of its athletic program; (8) government aid is important in all the public universities (42.9 percent at Florida, 26 percent at Alabama–Tuscaloosa, and 28.4 percent at Montclair State), but is not at the private universities (although it is undoubtedly significant in government sponsored research); (9) auxiliary services (a catch-all for a variety of service functions performed at all institutions, including such matters as housing, food services, parking, book stores, etc.) are a significant item of both revenue and expenditure at all schools, with the possible exception of Miami; and (10) auxiliary services appears generally to be a net producer of surpluses at the public universities, but a net expense at the private institutions (in absolute dollar terms).

We noted that Florida and Alabama–Tuscaloosa were included because they are elite athletic powers, yet profoundly different as research institutions. Florida is among the nation's top tier as a research university (and is a member of AAU, the premier group of research schools), while Alabama–Tuscaloosa is not an AAU member. At Florida, sponsored research amounted to 37 percent of total revenue ($673 million), but at Alabama it amounted to 11.6 percent ($65 million). On the expenditure side, Florida amounted to 25.4 percent ($461 million) for sponsored research against 5.3 percent ($26.1 million) at Alabama. The disparity is startling, and goes to institutional missions and goals. Alabama's Crimson Tide is a major source of pride and institutional support from alumni, state, and student body. What this means implicitly in terms of its academic input of resources and output of informed graduates becomes a troubling issue. One hopes that a credible, worthwhile education is received, due to a clear emphasis on teaching, minus the pressure for research prestige. Unhappily, one is left wondering. At Florida, however, one need not worry, although in past years there was evidence of unsavory actions in its athletic recruiting and the coddling of athlete misbehavior. The Gator Nation boasts that its championship teams are held to high behavioral standards, and that admission to the university requires meeting standards prevailing at other prestigious academic institutions.

Top sports programs do not compel compromising academic standards, although history suggests otherwise. Hopefully, as public awareness grows that allowing inferior standards of study and behavior are not compatible with university goals, or the well-being of both coddled athletes and society, NCAA's enforcement of its rules will hopefully improve the condition of university sports programs. We are not holding our breath.

Notes

1. *The Chronicle of Higher Education, Almanac Issue*, 2011–2012, August 20, 2011, 20.
2. The Annual Report on the Economic Status of the Profession, 2012–2013, *Academe*, AAUP, March–April, 8,16.
3. David W. Breneman and Chester E. Finn, Jr., eds., *Public Policy and Private Higher Education*, The Brookings Institution, Washington, DC, 1978, vii–viii.
4. *The Chronicle of Higher Education*, May 1, 2009, A16.
5. University of Oregon, University Relations, website: Public and Government Affairs. http://advancement.uoregon.edu/node/3
6. Ibid.
7. *The Chronicle of Higher Education, Almanac Issue, 2011–2012*, August 20, 2011, 10.
8. *The Chronicle of Philanthropy,* August 4–5, 2005, B, B1, B3.
9. Ibid.
10. Ibid.
11. *The Chronicle of Higher Education, Almanac Issue, 2011–2012*, August 26, 2011, 8.

Chapter 7

Conflicts of Interest and Division I Sports

A. Conflicts of Interest:
Nature and a Guide to Policy

1. Definition and Implications

A conflict of interest exists whenever a decision maker is exposed to an external influence or pressure that affects her or his decision, other than the critical criterion of the best interest of the institution she or he serves. In an academic institution, with power distributed among board, president (including provost and/or chancellor, if present), deans, chairpersons, and tenure-track faculty, conflicts of interest can arise as they address their respective responsibilities to the institution. These conflicts are not only material in nature. They are also moral, posing the issue of choice between right and wrong. They can present also the issue of individual gain as opposed to general well-being. About a century ago, Thomas Nixon Carver, a Harvard professor, wrote a book titled *Essays in Social Justice*. It contained a chapter in which he discussed the tendency of human beings to act in their own self-interest. But he noted an intriguing extension involving a preference for those close to an individual (family, tribe, sect, and so on) as opposed to those outside the group (he termed this *propinquity*). A possible anomaly arises: given a strong sense of loyalty to these others, an individual may subsume her or his benefit to advance the benefit of the group. We call this generosity. To recognize this possibility is to glimpse the complexity of conflict-of-interest issues.

Academic institutions are not medieval monasteries, secluded and largely separate from the external world. They are instead vibrant centers of learning, engaged in manifold interactions with the world at large. Today that world extends far beyond them, reaching across oceans to embrace relationships with foreign cultures as well as governments. They work with industry at home and abroad, in research, education, and other areas. In fiscal year 2008, universities issued 4,438 licenses to companies and other external entities granting them the right to use inventions resulting from university-led research. Further, universities applied for more than 10,800 patents. Academic inventions in such areas as medicine, plant genetics, and alternative energy, led to the creation of 549 spinoff companies. Also in fiscal 2008, revenue from licensing generated $2.4 billion in revenue for 156 universities and their inventors. The lion's share of this activity was accounted for by four research universities (the figures could fluctuate from year to year, so that the lead position would change for specific institutions): Northwestern, the University of California system, Columbia, and New York University. Northwestern received over $824 million in licensing income, formed 4 startup companies, executed 28 licenses, made 158 new patent applications, received 32 US patents, and spent a little over $368 million on research. The University of California system received $146.3 million in licensing revenue, Columbia took in $134.3 million, and NYU received $104.3 million. These data provide some indication of the scale of university research that is applied to commercial enterprise.[1]

Although this has positive outcomes for society, a lurking danger for the academic institution is the possible distortion of research motivation and faculty priorities as they assess their institutional responsibilities. Other potential conflict-of-interest situations include faculty engaged as consultants to industry, providing expertise to in-house research, advising on organizational and financial problems, and/or providing student interns (often without compensation, which raises a legal issue as to whether the interns must be paid at least minimum wages). Perhaps more important, there is direct industry funding of research conducted in the university, or externally but with direct compensation to participating faculty. We noted elsewhere the potential for distorting research data and results in favor of the sponsor's products, as well as the encroachment on the faculty members' time and commitment to the university. Put differently, the university has an enlarged responsibility to make sure that these relationships do not undermine its research or institutional mission, e.g., by creating a situation where monetary or other personal considerations improperly influence a faculty member's professional judgment. Of course, these constrictions apply no less to all university employees having decision-making authority.

Some other examples of conflicts of interest are: (1) monetary or other enticements offered by parties seeking to sell products or services to the university or college; most likely involving board members and/or top administrators; (2) monetary or other enticements offered by parties seeking the admission of unqualified students to the institution's degree programs (a public perception more widely accepted than is probably warranted, and a subject inviting hot debate over affirmative action programs); (3) nepotism (hiring and granting tenure to the spouse of a hotly recruited prospect, even though the spouse is less qualified than desired); and (4) monetary or other enticements by parties seeking the prestige of board membership, honorary degrees, or other awards.

Conflicts of interest cannot be wished away. Their existence is a stubborn reality. To contain them, by achieving a substantial measure of control, academic institutions adopt conflict-of-interest policies. Such policies are by now probably universal. In the case of public universities and colleges, in addition to individual institutional policies, there may be state laws dealing with conflicts of interest. In the case of private universities and colleges, there will be individual institutional policies. There also may be policies existing at the external funding sources (e.g., the federal government) that will be relevant.

2. Adoption of a Conflict-of-Interest Policy

A fundamental component of a policy must be a clear statement as to the primary and over-riding commitment of the faculty member or administrator to the institution. Whenever an employee's commitment to an external activity conflicts with her or his commitment of time and energy to teaching and service, as well as to research, this conflict is intolerable and must be removed. While not necessarily in order of importance, other basic principles to be clearly stated in a policy are: (1) transparency; (2) an acknowledgment of the acceptability of external activities, whether funded or not, that require some time from faculty or administrator, so long as they do not pose a conflict of commitment; and (3) any external activities that involve use of university resources and/or facilities must also be supportive of university teaching and service, as well as research.

There are two aspects of transparency; first, the externally sponsored activity must not in any way inhibit an open intellectual environment, embracing the freedom to publish the results of research; and, second, disclosure, i.e., the activity must be known to and approved by the university. Disclosure is insured when any external funding must be received by the university, and then be disbursed and recorded by the university's appropriate financial office. There may also be external payments that are not prohibited by the policy: amounts sufficiently small to be deemed not corrupting (embracing also gifts and/or social invitations to dinner, and so on). In the State of California, state law sets the amount at $500; above that sum there must be disclosure. The conflict may also be specified as involving "a significant financial interest." Such an interest doesn't necessarily have to be held directly by the faculty member or administrator. It can be and usually is, extended to include the spouse and/or a child of the employee. The financial interest is also broader than any direct payment of money. It can include a management or consultative arrangement involving the spouse and/or child, as well as any stock/equity holding in a sponsoring company exceeding some permissible amount (perhaps 5 percent, or $10,000).

Another area where the university's or college's best interests may be compromised involves the purchase of goods and services. Research universities, especially those with medical schools and teaching hospitals, are very large economic entities, with annual budgets aggregating billions of dollars. Their expenditures for goods and services offer opportunities for favoritism in dealings with suppliers, whether influenced by material or other enticements, or due simply to social friendships. Consequently, the conflict-of-interest policy should include explicit statements defining prohibited dealings. The statement should be especially careful to rule out any purchases from employees and their close relatives unless there has been prior disclosure and review, and it has been determined that the goods and services are not available from alternative business sources, or from the institution's own resources.

3. Implementation of Policy

Publishing a conflict-of-interest policy does not, by itself, minimize the problem. The ultimate test resides in the implementation of the policy, the organizational structure and documentary records that enforce the policy. We suggest an arrangement that establishes an independent committee to review, recommend approval or disapproval, and oversee situations where a potential or actual conflict of interest exists, as well as university administrative offices that will handle and disburse funds. In particular, the committee should make sure that research proposals meet the university's standards in research and teaching, involvement of students, and disclosure of scientific data. Normally, a sponsored research project will have a principal investigator, who will be associated with an academic department.

The committee would work with the principal investigator, to achieve:

1. disclosure of all related financial interests, including those in any publications resulting from the research;
2. independent monitoring of the research;
3. alterations of the research plan; and
4. termination of any relationship that creates a conflict of interest.

The committee would be appointed by the president or chancellor, i.e., the internal administrative leader of the institution, with advice and recommendations from designated members of the tenured faculty who are members of the senate (to ensure input from the units comprising the institution, with rotation of the members to keep the size of the committee effective). The membership should also include an ex-officio, non-voting member from the office charged with responsibility for handling the funds received from external sponsors (commercial, government, foundation, and so on), to enhance liaison. Additionally, there has to be an office to provide staff support for the committee. The office would design forms that describe and disclose any conflicts of interest. Its staff would also track and monitor the progress of the research project. Committee decisions would be sent to the president or chancellor for final review and agreement.

4. Technology Transfer (Inventions and Patents)

Passage of the Bayh-Dole Act in 1980 opened the doors to the commercialization of university-generated inventions. It opened also a substantial new revenue stream. Inherent in the situation was the question: what policy should apply to the distribution of the royalties generated by university research and teaching activities? Profit was not the ultimate goal, so the use and distribution of resulting revenues needed to be spelled out, and, more importantly, needed to be supportive of the institution's primary and over-riding knowledge goals. Applicable policies and their implementation had to be capable of controlling tendencies among faculty, administrators, and/or staff to become involved in conflicts of interest. Instead of the institution itself entering into commercial enterprise for profit, it would typically license its patents to outside business firms. The relationships among those firms and university employees had to be consistent with the purposes of the institution.

In any case, patents granted to universities mushroomed between 1965 and 1992 (mostly after 1980), according to Rebecca Henderson, Adam B. Jaffe, and Manuel Trajtenberg.[2] The authors observed that, in 1965, just 96 US patents were granted to 28 US universities or related institutions. In 1992, almost 1500 patents were granted to over 150 US universities or related institutions. They suggested further that the increase resulted from an increased propensity to seek patents, perhaps resulting in an associated increase in the rate-of-knowledge transfer to the private sector that was beneficial. It was also a source of substantial income to the universities, as well as a tempting target for hackers seeking to invade university computer systems (more about this in chapter 8).

Given that background, it is no mystery that academic institutions promulgated invention and patent policies designed to prevent conflicts of interest, by spelling out purpose, relationships, implementation structures, and distribution of royalty revenues. Yale University's is a good example. It opens with a statement encouraging the discovery of patentable inventions, followed by statements as to purpose, procedures, division of royalties, etc. The purpose of the policy is twofold: (a) to assure that the patentability and practicality of inventions will be evaluated by qualified people, and (b) to define the remuneration of inventor or inventors. Review and implementation of the policy is put into the hands of a committee on cooperative research, patents, and licensing (comprised of faculty and administrators) and an office of cooperative research (under a director). Inventors are required to assign all rights to inventions and patents to the university, unless it opts not to exercise that right. If the university does participate, it will seek to enter into an appropriate licensing agreement with a business firm or other suitable entity to commercialize the invention.

The division of the royalties is spelled out in some detail. All royalties must go first to cover any out-of-pocket expenses incurred by the university (the royalty arrangement may be expressed either in absolute dollar terms or as a percentage of gross royalty income), plus 10 percent of gross royalty receipts for the general support of the office of cooperative research. If the royalty stream exceeds the budget of that office, then the residue becomes net royalties. Net royalties are divided between the university and the inventor(s) according to this formula: the first $100,000 is divided 50-50 between the inventor and the university for the support of university research, the second $100,000 is divided 60% to the university and 40% to the inventor, any amount greater than $200,000 is divided 70% to the university and 30% to the inventor. The university, at its discretion, can, in lieu of cash, distribute equity to the inventor, or permit the outside licensee to distribute the equity. Net royalties are used to support general research, if not prohibited by any contract provision, and are allocated by the provost. All inventions by university employees, including those not covered by the foregoing provisions, must be reported to the university. If no university facilities or resources, including any job-related activities by the inventor, were used in producing the invention, all royalty rights belong to the employee, e.g., consulting arrangements unrelated to university facilities or job-related duties. Any outside contracts involving exceptions must be submitted to the president or the provost. An interesting sidelight to the policy is the OCR program for Technology Commercialization Internships. They are offered to PhD students or post-doctoral people in Life, Physical Sciences or Engineering, as well as to Law and MBA students, offering practical exposure to qualified students, and thereby enhancing the university's teaching mission.

Despite carefully drawn policy statements, some problems have arisen. A particularly significant one involves Stanford University. The university seeks to reclaim a series of patents it lost because one of its employee inventors assigned his ownership rights to a company as part of a consulting contract. Stanford and more than a dozen other research universities, along with the American Council on Education, are fighting a federal appeals court ruling that grants ownership to the company. The universities argue that the ruling could "cloud" their titles to thousands of federally funded inventions, which they maintain would be contrary to Congress's intent and the public interest. The universities and the ACE have asked the US Supreme Court to take up the case.[3]

B. Compensation Differences, Perceptions of Inequity, and External Markets

1. Compensation Differences

Examination of compensation data quickly reveals differentials reflecting a number of variables, depending on the basis of the comparison. Approached from this angle, we can identify these sources of difference: (1) rank, viz., endowed chair holder professor, professor, associate professor, assistant professor, instructor, and so on; (2) discipline, looked at broadly (humanities, business, medicine, law, etc.) or more narrowly (English and Sociology, or Finance and Marketing, or Internal Medicine and Neurosurgery, or Constitutional Law and Corporate Law, etc.); (3) type of institution, i.e., non-profit (public or private), and further categorized as doctoral, masters, or baccalaureate college; (4) geographic area or region; (5) gender; and (6) race or ethnicity. This listing is not exhaustive; other bases of comparison may be employed, depending on the objective of the examiner.[4]

Generally speaking, compensation is related directly to rank, which will occasion no surprise. It varies also by discipline, by substantial amounts, with business, medicine, and law receiving more than the humanities, social work, and education. These differences, especially those between business and the humanities, are a fruitful source of perceptions of inequity. Private institutions pay better than public ones, but this is conditioned also by whether they are doctoral (research) or not. A public research university will likely have a better compensation structure than a private baccalaureate institution. But, when comparing doctoral institutions, the opposite is true, and public universities are disadvantaged. Comparing all professorial ranks in public, as against private ones, the relative disadvantage increased from 2006–2007 to 2012–2013. For full professors, the comparative disadvantage rose from about 28% to 36%. For associate professors, it increased from about 18% to 28%. And for assistant professors, it rose from about 19% to 24%. The comparative disadvantage is markedly less in master's and baccalaureate institutions.[5]

Examining average salary differentials for 2009–2010 by discipline, we discover that if we take the average salary of a full professor of English language and literature as a norm, the average salaries of full professors in other disciplines varied widely around that norm. Specifically, the average salaries of full professors of fine arts were 12.4 percent less than those in English language and literature. At the other end of the spectrum, full professors of engineering received 25.2 percent more. Full professors of computer and information sciences received 28.4 percent more. But full professors of economics got 41.2 percent more; while business administration got 50.9 percent, and lawyers topped the list at 59.5 percent more.[6] If we compare the median salary differentials between university presidents and full professors, we find, again, that private institutions do better.[7] See Table 7-1.

Table 7-1

Comparison of Median Presidential and Full Professor Salaries (2010–2011)

Category	Ratio		Dollars	
	Public	Private	Public	Private
Doctoral	3.66	3.99	400,000	565,125
Master's	3.03	3.66	259,404	325,000
Bachelor's	2.66	3.39	201,660	257,500

Regional compensation differentials, given comparability in type of institution, show the northeast of the country as best compensated, at least in nominal terms. After adjustment for regional differences in the cost of living, the real differential would probably be reduced, but not eliminated. Gender differences are a fertile source of tension and litigation, but the trend is toward their long-term reduction. Race or ethnicity differentials, where they exist (in predominantly black institutions), attract attention, but they will hopefully be reduced and overcome with time, increased resources, and improved educational standards.[8]

Looking at salary differentials in doctoral institutions, by rank, we find that professors in private not-for-profit universities averaged $157,282 in 2010–11, while those in public universities averaged $118,054. The averages for associate professors, respectively, were $99,404 and $81,266. Assistant professors received $86,189 and $69,777, while instructors made $59,419 and $46,300.[9] The differentials are significant, both in terms of rank and type of institution.

Gender differentials are available for all institutions with academic ranks, a much broader classification than the one above. In addition to differentials reflecting rank and type of institution, male professors in *private* universities averaged $133,228 and women $116,182. Male associate professors averaged $85,593 and women $79,091; while male assistant professors averaged $72,667, as against $66,246 for women. Male instructors averaged $54,380, compared to $51,720. In *public* universities, male professors averaged $109,180 and women $96,219. Male associate professors averaged $77,792 and women $72,655. Male assistant professors received $66,091 and women $61,801. Instructors showed men averaging $46,015, but here the pattern was broken, with women averaging $46,859. Perhaps this is a portent of the future, but only time and a much deeper analysis of the several variables at work could provide an answer. In the meantime, the reality of gender differentials is inescapable.

Regional differentials are also significant. Looking again at all institutions with academic rank, including all ranks in the computations, we find the highest average salaries in the New England states, with $93,770. The Pacific coast states are next with $89,741. In descending order, we find the Middle Atlantic states at $87,926; the South Atlantic states at $77,405; the East North Central states at $77,057; the Mountain states at $74,872; the West South Central states at $74,537; the West North Central states at $72,336; and the East South Central at $68,235.[10] Remember that the regional figures are very broad and cover a wide range of institutions; consequently, substantial research institutions can be found in low salaried regions.

Texas is an interesting case, because it was not impacted severely by the 2008-09 recession, given its wealth in oil and natural gas resources. In fact, Texas moved to improve the research stature of its leading universities in those years, using its relative financial strength to lure outstanding scholars to relocate. From 2005 to 2010, Texas increased spending on higher education by more than 34 percent. In the 2008–10 period, it increased appropriations by 8 percent. It has its eyes on New York and California, which have, respectively, 7 and 9 universities that are members of the prestigious Association of American Universities (total membership is 63). Texas has only 3 members of the AAU, though its population ranks second after California.[11]

We know that traditionally black universities suffer generally from greater financial pressure than their white counterparts, but we do not have specific data. We do not know about racial differentials within specific institutions, although we would guess that they are absent at such prestigious universities as Harvard.

Presidents and deans have to manage these differentials, but some may prove more intractable than others. Differences by discipline seem the most difficult, because they are closest to faculty perceptions of inequity, since they confront faculty in the same location and institution. Of course, the same is true of gender differences. Of the two, differentials by discipline may be more difficult because they are impacted heavily by external labor markets. Put differently, well-paid external (non-academic) market opportunities are available to attorneys, physicians, and business professors, as compared with English professors, social work educators, education professors, or scholars of ancient classics. This is the sad reality, and it has to be reflected in the budgetary decisions made by academic leaders, which is not to say that they should eschew seeking funds to support the humanities; rather, they should support them with vigor.

2. Perceptions of Inequity

Faculty in the disadvantaged disciplines perceive a grievous inequity in the disparity between their compensation levels and those of their colleagues in business, law, and medicine, but the sense of injustice is probably greatest in the comparison with business. After all, law and medicine have long been taught at the graduate level, while business is frequently offered at the undergraduate level. Perhaps more to the point, traditionally the Arts & Sciences regarded business curricula, students, and faculty as intellectually inferior in the academic pecking order. But that changed radically after the publication of the Gordon-Howell and the Pierson reports on business education in 1959. The Gordon-Howell study was sponsored by the Ford Foundation. The Pierson study was sponsored by the Carnegie Foundation. That sponsorship, plus the damning and negative nature of the two reports' conclusions, gave particular force to their impact.

Business education at the university level underwent a major revolution in curriculum, standards for student admissions, and standards for faculty tenure-track appointments and promotion. Within three decades, the academic stature of the business schools rose dramatically, frequently surpassing that of the Arts & Sciences. The latter, which had traditionally been the hallmark of academic quality, experienced a concurrent debasement of the intellectual rigor that had formerly characterized their disciplines (particularly in the social sciences, as contrasted with the natural sciences). In fact, in the NYU self-survey of 1956, which became the master plan for the transformation of the university, one blunt recommendation called for the termination of any undergraduate division that did not approximate the standards applied by the Arts and Sciences College.

Despite these earth-shaking changes, the social sciences professor (excepting economists), with her or his PhD, feels that the intellectual rigor represented by that degree makes it the equal of the PhD held by professors in the business faculty. Given that history and perception, it is understandable that professors in the social sciences would feel aggrieved by differences in compensation between those disciplines. The situation is somewhat ameliorated by university establishment of salary structures that apply dollar brackets for each rank across the several schools and colleges of the institution. Differences within each bracket might be established to allow greater flexibility for faculty associated with graduate programs, an arrangement less likely to arouse resentment and resistance among less-favored faculty. Of course, inter-disciplinary differentials may still exist within a given salary structure, due to uneven distribution and clustering of compensation data across the disciplines. Thus for each rank, the average compensation within the rank could differ between the business and the social sciences faculties. In any event, external markets (available alternative employment opportunities offering superior compensation) will have an impact on compensation within the university.

To this point, we have not mentioned the relationship of professorial compensation—especially tenured full professors—to that for university presidents. In recent years, presidential compensation has surged, and leaders, in both public and private institutions, are now receiving packages of $1 million or more per year. Perhaps the most striking cases involved E. Gordon Gee at Ohio State ($1,992,221), Michael D. McKinney at Texas A&M University system ($1,966,347), and Graham B. Spanier at Pennsylvania State University at University Park ($1,068,763). Gee and Spanier are now ex-presidents; the former brought down by a case of foot-in-mouth disease, and the latter by the Sandusky football scandal at Penn State. In any case, the surge has attracted the attention and opprobrium of the professoriate, especially in the straightened financial circumstances of the Great Recession.

C. External Markets: The Special Challenge of Division I Sports Programs

Economics embraces a concept known as opportunity cost, i.e., the loss (cost) experienced when a person chooses to surrender one opportunity in favor of another one. If we assume that most human beings generally prefer better compensation to poorer compensation, allowing for equivalence in other conditions, then the less favored alternative is under pressure to meet the competition of the more favored alternative. Given that context, it follows that an academic institution is under pressure to pay business faculty more than faculty in the humanities. There is a caveat: life in the Academy is presumably more pleasant and leisurely than in any Wall Street bank, or in any profit-seeking commercial enterprise. The difference in life style can account for some difference in compensation. But the difference cannot be too great, because it will fester and poison the spirit as time passes. We conclude that the academic leader has "wiggle room" in the compensation structure, but ultimately must deal with the pressure from external markets.

A special compensation challenge confronts the university or college president whose institution has a Division I football and/or basketball program. In those sports, the universities' or colleges' teams serve as minor leagues for the professional sports, and are big business. It avails nothing that the academic may be dismayed by huge compensation packages for coaches, and unsavory practices in recruitment and progress to a degree by students on athletic scholarships. Division I football and basketball involve important considerations, from both revenue and reputation aspects. Winning teams get huge publicity that helps attract non-athletic students and tuition revenue. Also, they fill large stadiums that produce additional revenue, and energize alumni support for facilities and endowment building. Unhappily, there is a profound institutional conflict of interest between the university's or college's academic mission and its support of top-flight athletic programs (especially Division I).

An indication of the magnitude of big-time college sports was provided by an analysis by *The New York Times* of the ten athletic conferences with major football programs: the Southeast; the Big-Ten; the Pacific 12; the Big 12; the Mountain West; the Sun Belt; the Conference USA; the American; the Atlantic Coast; and the Mid-American. These conferences embraced 127 colleges and universities, respectively numbering 14, 14, 12, 10, 12, 11, 14, 12, 15, and 13. The figures are based on conference press announcements, relate to a forecast for 2015, and may be subject to change.[12]

The New York Times, in another, this time front-page, article, exposed the degree to which commercial interests and incentives have come to control big-time university sports, especially football. In blunt language, the *Times* said:

> Far beyond televising games, ESPN has become the chief impresario of college football. By infusing the sport with billions of dollars it pays for television rights—more than $10 billion on college football in the last five years alone—ESPN has become both puppet-master and king-maker, arranging games, setting schedules, and bestowing the gift of nationwide exposure on its chosen universities, coaches and players.
>
> The money and programming focused on college football by ESPN, as well as its competitors, has transformed the game, creating professionalized sports empires in the midst of academic institutions.
>
> At a time of rising tuition and fiscal struggles, the millions of dollars that flow to the top athletic departments are, with few exceptions, used to enhance athletics, not academics. Celebrity coaches earn many times more than college presidents, and even teams at financially strained public universities train in lavish facilities financed by donors and corporate sponsors.
>
> In the chase for money and exposure, college football, once a quaint drama of regional rivalries played out on autumn Saturday afternoons, has become a national sport played throughout the week, intruding on class schedules and even on exams.[13]

In a follow-up, front page article the next day, *The New York Times* focused on the connection between ESPN and the University of Louisville, which has become a major big-time sports school. The story captured the complexity and seductive nature of the sports–academic interaction. It said:

> Louisville's ascent is a case study of how an institution of higher learning can become all but inextricably conjoined with ESPN, an institution of higher profits. It illustrates not only ESPN's power to make

kings among athletic programs, but also how profoundly its presence can affect an entire university and its institutional priorities.

Athletic acclaim, of course, was never supposed to be an end in itself at Louisville. The idea was to jump-start a transformation of the university as a whole. These days, the 30-second advertising spots shown during ESPN telecasts of Cardinals games announce the university's academic advances to the world: the students who perform better, graduate more often and more readily choose to live on campus. The 36 total Fullbright scholarships in 2010, 2011 and 2012 are more, university officials point out, than the total at Dartmouth or M.I.T. (note: disregarding comparative enrollments at these institutions) The swelling research budget and the fivefold increase, since 1998, in the number of endowed professorships and chairs. All this helped by the donations that have increasingly poured in: about $1 billion since 2004.[14]

The NCAA (National Collegiate Athletic Association), responding hesitantly to the trend of events, has tightened somewhat its regulations, as well as their implementation, respecting recruitment of athletes and their academic progress and behavior. The NCAA has a powerful financial motive to uphold the integrity of Division I sports programs in its member universities and colleges. In April 2010, the Association reached a 14-year, $10.86 billion agreement ($776 million per year) with CBS Sports and Turner Broadcasting System to televise the men's basketball tournament. That deal covers only basketball. But scandals continue to surface, most recently at Penn State, the University of North Carolina at Chapel Hill, and other institutions. These scandals compromise the place of Division I sports in academic institutions, and threaten the NCAA itself.

1. Academic Institutions and Division I Sports Programs

The role of Division I sports in a number of prestigious academic institutions demands a more detailed look. Sports programs are not a declared priority at the graduate and doctoral levels, but they are often of major importance at the undergraduate level. Historically, large sports programs were major aspects of life at such old and esteemed institutions as the Ivies, especially in football and basketball (Harvard, Yale, Princeton, Columbia, Pennsylvania, Cornell, as well as Chicago and others). But after World War II, they were downgraded. In those schools, they are no longer big-time. Other universities and colleges continue to have major sports programs. They compete with the professional sports teams for coaches, and with each other for players good enough to aspire to professional careers. This competition with the external market explains the huge disparity between the compensation packages received by top football coaches in Division I institutions, when compared with the compensation packages of presidents. For example, an article *in The Wall Street Journal* observed:

> College-football coaches have it pretty good these days. Some might say too good. Five years ago, there were three coaches making $2 million a year in the college ranks. This season there will be 21. Alabama's second-year coach, Nick Saban, makes six times more than the president of the university. And it's not just premier programs paying huge salaries: Southern Methodist's new coach, June Jones, will earn about $2 million per season—four times what his predecessor made. . . . Four coaches were known to have compensation topping $3 million per season—Alabama's Mr. Saban, Oklahoma's Bob Stoops, Florida's Urban Meyer and Iowa's Kirk Ferentz.[15]

But, the leading coach was Peter Carroll of the University of Southern California, with a 2006–2007 total compensation package worth $4.4 million.[16] Carroll has since left, before the USC sports program suffered penalties for infractions of NCAA rules. The penalties, severe when compared to those of the past, cost USC a two-year ban on participation in future bowl games, and the loss of thirty athletic scholarships. The loss of athletic scholarships significantly impairs USC's recruitment capability for attracting promising athletes.

The Chronicle of Higher Education reported data about six major collegiate athletic conferences: Atlantic Coast, Big East, Big Twelve, Big Ten, Pacific Ten, and Southeastern. Of particular interest is data indicating progress in the academic performance of student athletes in meeting or exceeding the NCAA (National Collegiate Athletic Association) minimum Academic Performance Standard. The data presented in table 7-2 indicates the percentage improvement achieved in each of the six conferences between 2005 and 2009.[17]

Table 7-2

Percentage of Student Athletes Meeting or Exceeding NCAA Minimum Academic Progress Rate for Six Major Athletic Conferences (2005–2009)

Conference	2005	2006	2007	2008	2009
Atlantic Coast	81	90	92	96	96
Big East	76	78	76	85	91
Big Twelve	41	54	61	78	87
Big Ten	65	72	81	86	91
Pacific Ten	38	62	72	77	92
Southeastern	44	56	67	73	79

The NCAA is having some effect on the behavior of the athletic departments in the schools covered by the conferences; all are improving in respect to NCAA's minimum academic progress rate. But the effect is mixed among the conferences. The Atlantic Conference, leading the compliance parade over the entire five-year period, appears to have been most conscious of the academic performance of its student athletes. The degree of improvement is most marked in the Pacific Ten and Big Twelve conferences. But the Southeastern Conference is plainly the laggard. It is also the conference with the greatest concentration of highly-paid football coaches, and the richest in generating funding. We do not mean to imply a necessary causal relationship between monetary incentives and relative laxity with regard to academic performance by its student athletes. But the pressure for athletic success is probably intense, and a factor that is receiving attention in the conference. In this case, NCAA pressure helps stimulate extensive and expensive special remedial and support programs for student athletes. And it appears that some student athletes, who would have been admitted to the universities in former years are no longer enrolled. So there is progress, but it is far from being meaningful.

NCAA's efforts to raise player eligibility standards is not easy sailing. For example, in May 2013, its Division I Board of Directors decided to roll back a change in a new eligibility requirement for freshmen athletes, which was to become effective in 2016. Originally, the minimum grade point average (GPA) was raised from 2.0 to 2.3, plus a minimum SAT score of 1080 or ACT score of 93, as well as stiffer rules for core courses required in high school. Now, players with a 2.3 GPA will need only a 900 SAT score, or a 75 ACT score. Players who failed to meet the new requirement would be barred from playing in their first year.[18]

Note should be taken of the work of the Knight Commission on Intercollegiate Athletics. In its two decades of effort to advise the NCAA about introducing regulations that would advance attention by Division I sports programs to academic standards applied to student athletes, it has had some effect. The Commission suggested that TV revenues be distributed based on the academic success of student athletes—e.g., graduating at least half of an institution's players—not only on victories and appearances. William Kirwan, co-chairman of the Commission and chancellor of Maryland's university system, remarked, "The situation we're in right now is basically a financial race to generate more and more money to invest in intercollegiate athletics, and it's a time when our institutions are under such incredible pressure to maintain the integrity of their academic programs."[19]

Since the Southeastern Conference is the current athletic powerhouse of the collegiate universe, it requires additional scrutiny. In particular, data comparing expenditures for academic instruction and for athletic programs are both interesting and instructive. *The Chronicle of Higher Education* has published relevant data, and it is presented in Table 7-3.[20]

Look at the five universities that spend over $70 million a year on their athletic programs: Florida, Tennessee (Knoxville), Louisiana State (Baton Rouge), Alabama (Tuscaloosa), and Georgia. Money talks! Those schools are known nationally as football powerhouses, and Florida and Tennessee are also leaders in basketball. In fact, these two universities outspend the other three, on average, by $19 million a year. And Florida alone tops the list with its $98.2 million. The real story, however, stands out starkly when the athletic expenditure figures are compared with those shown for instruction. Florida's athletic expenditure is outweighed by the $548.5 million it spends on instruction (which excludes its large expenditures on research). Put differently, Florida's athletic budget amounts to slightly less than 18% of its instruction spending. The University of Alabama provides a sharply contrasting picture. It spends $74.9 million on its athletic programs, compared with $168.5 million spent on instruction. The former figure amounts to slightly less than 45% of the latter. It appears that one can legitimately inquire as to the institutional priorities

Table 7-3

Comparative University Expenditures on Athletics and Instruction
Southeastern Conference—SEC
(Reported in September 2009)

University	University Expenditures in Millions of Dollars			
	(Millions of $)	(Millions of $)	% Increase	% Increase
	Athletic	Instruction	Athletic	Instruction
Georgia	70.5	212.1	57	12
Alabama-Tuscaloosa	74.9	168.5	50	32
So. Carolina-Columbia	64.5	226.9	50	28
Arkansas-Fayetteville	62.7	108.4	42	14
Auburn	69.8	172.5	38	5
LA State-Baton Rouge	76.3	221.9	37	12
Florida	98.2	548.5	34	20
Kentucky	67.8	258	31	11
Vanderbilt	45.5	657.2	24	47
Tennessee-Knoxville	87.4	412.4	22	14
Mississippi	34.8	105.1	21	22
Mississippi State	30.4	9.2	19	12
Total	**782.8**	**3180.7**	**36**	**22**

at Alabama (Tuscaloosa). Moving beyond the five universities considered so far, we take note of the University of Arkansas (Fayetteville), where spending on athletic programs amounts to slightly less than 58% of its outlays for instruction. Testing further the priorities of some of the schools in the SEC, we cast a glance at the relative increases in spending on athletics as against instruction. The University of Georgia fairly leaps into the forefront. Its spending on athletics increased by 57 percent, as compared with an increase of only 12 percent for instruction. Is there much room for argument as to its emphasis on achieving a leading place nationally for its athletic program, especially in football?

We have reserved any comment so far about Vanderbilt University, because it represents so dramatic a contrast to its fellow members in the SEC. The data show us a university that, while a member of the leading sports conference in the country, clearly places its primary institutional priority on its academic mission. Its $657.2 million spent on instruction dwarfs the $45.5 million expended for athletics. The latter figure represents only 7 percent of the former. Further emphasizing the point, Vanderbilt increased its large spending for instruction by 47 percent, while its outlay for athletics increased by 24 percent. One should keep in mind when interpreting these numbers, that large percentage changes are easiest when the absolute numbers underlying them are small. Another perspective is provided by the American Association of University Professors, which publishes extensive data for American higher education. The March-April 2008 issue of the Association's official publication, *Academe*, compared and analyzed data about the salaries of football coaches and full professors for the eleven Division I football conferences. The coaches' data were gathered by *USA Today*, which acquired contract data about 120 football coaches who lead top Division I teams in the 2007–2008 academic year. AAUP provided the professorial salary data.

> The data showed two years of average salaries for head football coaches, average salaries of full professors, and the ratio of the two for the eleven Division I football conferences. In 2007–08, the average salary of the coaches is $1,040,863, a 12.4% increase over the $925,683 average paid in 2006/07. By contrast, the average salary of full professors at these universities in 2007/08 is $104,523, 3.5% more than the $100,998 paid in 2006–07. In 2006–07, the average head football coach earned 9.2 times the average full professor's salary, that ratio increased to 10 this year. What does this say about the priorities of Division I universities? . . . [T]he national averages . . . mask substantial differences between conferences. In the Mid-American Conference, coaches this year are earning 2.4 times the average salary of full professors. . . . By contrast, this year head coaches in the Southeastern Conference are earning 18.6 times the salary of the full professors who carry out the primary functions of their institutions—teaching and research. Full professor average salaries are up 5.5 percent from last year but are dwarfed by the 36.4 percent increase in average head coach salaries.[21]

On April 28, 2013, *USA Today* reported the current salaries of the Division I head football coaches making $ 1 million or more per annum. Two, Nick Saban of Alabama (Tuscaloosa) and Mark Brown of Texas, were over $5 million; 3 were between $4 and $5 million (Bob Stoops of Oklahoma, Urban Meyer of Ohio State, and Les Miles of Louisiana State); 11 were between $3 million and $3.9 million; 36 were between $2 million and $2.9 million; 26 were between $1 million and $1.9 million; 30 were between $.5 million and $.9 million; and 16 were between $.35 million and $.89 million.[22] The *USA Today* analysis commented "For all of the TV money flowing to athletics departments in the best known conferences, only 22 athletics departments are self-support-ing, . . . (T)he majority get subsidies from the university, often through student fees."

A major justification for paying high salaries to head football coaches in Division I is that the programs generate profits that can be shared with other sports programs, as well as with academic programs. *Forbes,* in an analysis of the value and profitability of major football programs, pub-lished the data for the top 20 programs in 2012. The profitability ranged from $78 million for the University of Texas Longhorns to $24 million for the University of Wisconsin Badgers and the Ohio State Buckeyes. Considering the capital investment (stadiums, etc.) and annual budgets of these programs, the profitability appears modest. It is certainly not a deep well for the presumably benefited academic programs.[23]

An additional factor is the way the market works for coaches. They are typically represented by agents, who get a percentage of the value of the contract that is negotiated. Being skilled negotiators, and having a powerful motive to get as much as they can, they will protract negotia-tions and drive a hard bargain. The academic leader and her or his ath-letic director, pressed to achieve winning teams, is in the weaker bar-gaining position, which may explain part of the results we have portrayed.

The remuneration of head basketball coaches in Division I programs warrant particular attention. In June 2011, Charlie Zegers, formerly with About.Com, reported on the *Highest Paid Coaches in Basketball*. He provided data for 15 of the coaches, indicating average salaries ranging from Rick Pitino's (U. of Louisville) $7.5 million to Jim Boehelm's (Syracuse U.) $1 million plus. Two coaches were in the $4 million to $4.9 million range; two more were in the $3 million to $3.9 million range; six were in the $2 million to $2.9 million range; and four were in the $1 million to $1.9 million range.[24] The figures are not strictly comparable, because some institutions include items that others do not, e.g., advertising deals with apparel companies (sneakers). Also, public universities and colleges have to be more forthcoming than private ones. Clearly, basketball is a runner-up to football, but not nearly as financially lucrative. Not to worry! No tears need be shed for the basketball coaches.

Advocates for Division I sports programs point out that they stimulate large donations to the universities and colleges that participate. *The Chronicle of Higher Education* reported the results of a survey of athletics donations in major college sports programs, i.e., 73 colleges in the six leading conferences (Atlantic Coast Conference, Big East Conference, Big 12 Conference, Big Ten Conference, Pacific Ten Conference, Southeastern Conference).[25] Of particular interest was a table on page A-13 of that issue that compared the schools with the ten largest sports endowments with each school's overall endowment. It then converted that data to sports endowment per scholarship student athlete as contrasted with overall endowment per undergraduate student. The results are seen in Table 7-4.

Table 7-4

Sports Endowment per Scholarship Student-Athlete Compared With Overall Endowment per Undergraduate Student

School	Sports Endowment per Student Athlete	Overall Endowment per Undergraduate Student
Univ. of NC-Chapel Hill	$485,126	$122,784
Duke University	$444,594	$924,348
Boston College	$381,679	$169,380
Georgia Tech	$274,174	$128,028
Univ. of Virginia	$129,715	$289,740
Univ. of Washington	$147,368	$76,457
Univ. of Georgia	$126,551	$27,840
Penn. State Univ.	$109,756	$43,189
Univ. of Connecticut	$141,328	$20,672
Ohio State Univ.	$69,909	$59,632

Two comments seem in order: (1) in only two schools (Duke and Virginia) did the endowment per undergraduate student exceed that of the student-athletes; and (2) eight of the schools (including Georgia Tech in that group) are public institutions. In any case, the strength of sports programs in many schools, private as well as public, is a reality that academic administrators must deal with, as they work to uphold the quality and variety of the academic programs in their institutions.

The impact of the severe recession of 2008–2009 on sports programs warrants a comment. *The New York Times* reported the following facts:

> According to NCAA figures, a record 17,682 college teams competed in the 2007–8 academic year, 60 percent more than in 1981–82. During that time, the number of student-athletes grew 78 percent, to a record 412,768. . . . Yet only twice in the past two decades—in 1988–89 and 1997–98—has there been a net decline in the number of men's and women's athletic programs nationally.[26]

In an interview on his book, *Big Time Sports in American Universities*, Charles T. Clotfelter observed:

> For almost a century, big time college sports has been a wildly popular but consistently problematic part of American higher education. The challenges it poses to traditional academic values have been recognized from the start, but they have grown more ominous in recent decades, as cable television has become ubiquitous, commercial opportunities have proliferated, and athletic budgets have ballooned.

2. The Persistence of Scandals

Despite the efforts of the NCAA and its Knight commission, Division I sports scandals are like congealing tar: they seem impossible to remove. Year after year, the reputations of schools with big-time sports programs are sullied. Recent cases involved Penn State, the University of North Carolina-Chapel Hill, the University of South Carolina-Columbia, the University of Southern California, Stanford, Rutgers, the University of Miami, and others. The infractions are numerous and varied; admission of student athletes who are academically deficient, grade and course manipulation to maintain their eligibility to play, cover-up of illegal actions, e.g., sexual violations and drunkenness, improper payments and expensive gifts, violations by coaches (Sandusky at Penn State) and other academic officials involved with the athletic programs, and more. The problem is inherent and deep-seated.

3. A Solution?

William Casement, in an article excerpted from his book (*Making College Right: Heretical Thoughts and Practical Proposals*) spelled out a solution to the quandary of Division I sports in an academic setting. The fulcrum on which his proposals rest establishes that:

> *Teams that operate on a big-time model will be declared professional. All other teams are amateur.* This two-part structure replaces the present and more complicated NCAA . . . structure of Divisions IA, IAA, II, and III. Educational and non-educational interests are no longer tied together through nuancing—instead, they're clearly demarcated and left to follow their natural paths."[27]

As to specifics:

1. A professional team is owned by an entity outside of the school bearing its name; perhaps a coalition of alumni boosters, or a local business or community group. Profits belong to the ownership entity, with the school receiving a generous share. Losses are borne entirely by the ownership. Teams are free to make connections with major league professional teams, perhaps allowing part ownership.

2. Professional teams have no restrictions on how they obtain revenue (ticket sales, team uniforms and paraphernalia, advertising, etc.) Teams pay income taxes on their profits.

3. Ownership of athletic facilities can vary, but a stadium or arena (whether on or off campus) used mostly by a professional team should be owned by the team, or another outside entity.

4. Instead of athletic scholarships, players will be paid salaries based on their athletic skills and market demands. Players are not required to be students at the school whose team they play for. If they want to be students, they will receive no preference for their status as an athlete. They are free to enroll in any school, and they will probably attend classes in the off-season or part-time. Amateur players on college teams

will be welcome to try out for professional teams. If they make the team, however, they must understand that their professional commitment is primary, and will require limiting their college studies.

5. All teams that are not professional are designated as amateur. There are no athletic scholarships or other financial consideration for being an athlete. Playing seasons and off-season practices are carefully limited. Preference to varsity athletes in admission, given commonly today, will be largely eliminated, used only in connection with policies to achieve a diverse student body. Athletes accepted for admission to a college, should fall within its academic profile of accepted students as a whole. Highly selective colleges may balk, concerned by a lack of diversity in the student body, but they should be able to draw academically viable athletes. What they lose are star players who are under-qualified. The admissions restriction must be written carefully into NCAA regulations, and enforced through regular reviews of colleges' admissions office records.

6. The new system will apply to all sports, not just big-time football and basketball. The reason: all sports are subject to the same problems of exploiting athletes and draining the budget. Varsity athletes will use the same services as other students, i.e., no special housing, meals, or tutoring. Expenditures for athletics will be fully disclosed, and subject to a uniform accounting system monitored by the NCAA.

7. Finally, the NCAA will abandon its commercial function. No longer concerned with profits, its focus will be strictly on enforcing the rules of amateurism, since some schools and coaches may yearn for the old ways as means to achieve competitive advantages.

Will the proposals work? Can such a thorough overhaul of the existing system have a prospect of adoption? The questions are daunting. Large, powerful vested interests will be eviscerated. An entire infrastructure of physical facilities (housing, training, tutoring, etc.), representing large capital investments and named facilities honoring donors, will have to be made available to the general student body. Wealthy investor/supporters will have to be found to take over ownership of the schools' professional teams, with total responsibility for losses coupled with generously sharing profits, should there be any. The financial aspect of the proposals do not seem attractive: love for the game and the school would have to be major incentives. Perhaps the professional big-league teams of the National Football League and the National Basketball League would take over the teams, and set them up as minor league entities. In any case, the collision between Division I sports and the academic mission of universities and colleges needs to be confronted and resolved.

Dr. Casement's proposals do not seem to be a promising place to start. A solution will be the outcome rather of a law suit which has been working its way through the courts since 2009. It strikes at the heart of the NCAA's power; the billions of dollars it receives from TV networks for broadcasting Division I football and basketball games, as well as revenue from ads that use star athletes names and likenesses. *The NCAA has an exclusive contractual right to such use,* based on its requirement that student/athletes sign such an agreement as a precondition to eligibility to play. It is also a prerequisite to eligibility to athletic scholarships, etc. The lawsuit, filed by Mr. Ed O'Bannon, argues that this exercise is an illegal (antitrust) usurpation of the athletes' right to share in the resulting revenue. In June 2013, Michael Hausfeld, Mr. O'Bannon's lawyer, sought to extend the lawsuit into a class-action case. To date, 25 present and former student athletes have joined the O'Bannon lawsuit. The case is strong. It would add former athletes to O'Bannon's claim to share in the earnings stream that is the NCAA's lifeblood. In addition to the loss of future income, it would impose a large liability on the NCAA for its past actions. This adverse financial impact would compromise the power now exerted by the NCAA over "big-time" college sports programs, and enable true reforms that would erase the myth of "student/athletes" as amateurs rather than professional athletes. Once separated, players could be seen and treated as athletes, with no special claims as students. And a rich source of the scandals that have marred the reputations of big-time sports schools would have been eliminated.[28]

The NCAA has fought the O'Bannon lawsuit with vigor and tenacity, seeking to have the court dismiss the action. That effort has failed. US District Judge Claudia Wilken ruled against the NCAA. With additional complainants having joined O'Bannon, Judge Wilken let stand the plaintiffs contention that NCAA rules restrained competition. It seems clear that, as the O'Bannon lawsuit inches its way through the courts, it is having an impact on the NCAA. A significant sign of worry, if not desperation, is NCAA's consideration of creating "benefits," but not "payments," for student-athletes.[29] The word *payments* implies a commercial relationship. It is anathema to the NCAA, which clasps close to its heart the myth that big-time college sports is engaged in by amateurs, rather than professionals.

The NCAA's defense against the O'Bannon lawsuit was weakened also by the withdrawal from the case of its two co-defendants, EA Sports and Collegiate Licensing Company, both having settled with the plaintiffs for $40 million. Even *The New York Times* has waded into the controversy with an editorial titled "Fairness for College Athletes." The editorial stated:

> The amateur *model* in college sports is in serious trouble. . . . Under NCAA rules, student athletes may not receive compensation. . . . Instead of waiting to see what happens in court, the NCAA could move to settle. . . . But, for now, the NCAA remains obstinate and plans to keep fighting.[30]

Of course it will fight! The myth that student athletes are amateurs is its lifeblood and worth billions of dollars. That is a huge incentive to remain blind to reality. The blinders, however, are less total than they were. We note recent moves to restructure the governance of the NCAA by admitting students to two seats and voting rights on a proposed new 38-member NCAA legislative committee. Also considered is the possibility of membership on the potent Division I Board of Directors.

As recently as March 2014, the petition by football players at Northwestern University—one of America's leading research universities—to form a union, is of possibly equal significance. Led by Kain Colter, its recent quarterback, they filed a petition with the Chicago office of the National Labor Relations Board. The petition asked the Board to recognize the group (the College Athletes Players Association) as "employees," An older and larger group (the National College Players Association), with a membership of some 17,000, assumed leadership of the effort. The NCAA responded vigorously and negatively, as it did in fighting the O'Bannon lawsuit. But the NCAA lost the first round when Peter Sung Ohr, regional director of the NLRB's Chicago office, decided that the football players at Northwestern University were university employees subject to the employer's control. He decided that the scholarships they received constituted payments for providing football services to the university. The university plans to appeal. Also worthy of note is a federal antitrust lawsuit filed by a lawyer representing four college athletes. The NCAA's five largest conferences are the target of the lawsuit. The suit asserts that players' compensation (note the word *compensation*) has been illegally capped at the value of an athletic scholarship. While the petition and the lawsuit may not succeed eventually, they are another line of attack on the dominance of the NCAA. In the long-run, the odds are good that the NCAA will fracture, and the myth of the "student/athlete" in big-time sports will weaken and be supplanted by a more realistic model.

Perception is important. To athletic directors and NCAA officials, athletic programs are primary. The star football coaches, with their large compensation packages, as well as the athletes with their athletic scholarships, and the student body, along with alumni, state legislators and other avid supporters of sports, are eager to have winning teams. That is their mission, and they make it a large part of the university's mission. University presidents cannot, even if they want, do away with or simply and arbitrarily cut back existing major sports programs. We believe breaking the power of the NCAA and ESPN is the key to ending the scandals that have so soiled the academic enterprise.

Notes

1. *The Chronicle of Higher Education*, February 26, 2010, A25–26.
2. *Review of Economics and Statistics,* "Universities as a Source of Commercial Technology: A Detailed Analysis of University Patenting," 1998, 119–127.
3. *The Chronicle of Higher Education*, May 7, 2010, A3.
4. Ibid.
5. *Academe*, "Annual Report on the Economic Status of the Profession, 2012-2013," AAUP, March–April 2013, 16–17, 18, Figures 2, 3, 4.
6. *The Chronicle of Higher Education, Almanac Issue, 2011-2012*, August 26, 2011, 23.
7. *Academe*, "Annual Report on the Economic Status of the Profession," 2012–2013, AAUP, March–April 2013, 10.
8. *Academe*, March–April 2009, 25.
9. *The Chronicle of Higher Education, Almanac Issue*, 2011-2012, August 26, 2011, 22.
10. *The Chronicle of Higher Education*, April 16, 2010, A10.

11. *The Chronicle of Higher Education*, March 26, 2010, A1, 24.

12. *The New York Times,* Sports Section, November 30, 2013, B11.

13. James Andrew Miller, Steve Eder, and Richard Sandomir, "College Football's Biggest Player? ESPN," *The New York Times,* August 25, 2013, 1, SP 14P.

14. Steve Eder, Richard Sandomir, and Andrew Miller, "Louisville's Made-for-TV Sports Boom." *The New York Times,* August 26, 2013, A1, D4.

15. *The Wall Street Journal,* August 20, 2008, W, W1, W4.

16. *The Chronicle of Higher Education*, February 27, 2009, A1.

17. *The Chronicle of Higher Education*, September 4, 2009, A27.

18. Brad Wolverton, "NCAA's Easing of Eligibility Standards Concerns Some Professors," *The Chronicle of Higher Education*, May 3, 2013.

19. *The New York Times,* June 18, 2010, B14.

20. *The Chronicle of Higher Education*, September 4, 2009, A26.

21. *Academe*, March-April 2008, 11–13.

22. *USA Today,* "Coaches Hot Seat: Salaries and Contracts," April 28, 2013; and Erik Brady, Jodi Upton, and Steve Berkowitz, "Salaries for College Football Coaches Back on Rise," *USA Today*, April 28, 2013.

23. *Forbes,* "The Business of College Football" and "College Football's Most Valuable Teams," January 19, 2012 and April 28, 2013.

24. Charlie Zegers, "Highest Paid Coaches in Basketball," *About.Com: Basketball*, April 28, 2013.

25. *The Chronicle of Higher Education*, January 23, 2009, A1, A12–14, A16.

26. *The New York Times,* May 4, 2009, D1, 6.

Chapter 8

Service Functions: A Secondary Source of Threats to the Academic Mission

A. The Need for Support Services: The Growth Picture

For the past several decades, academic institutions have been significantly affected by huge technological developments as well as expanded functions and activities. These developments, functions, and activities did not affect them so significantly in times past. The expansion in functions, coupled with the requirements of new technologies and scientific research, required the employment of additional support staff. The numbers of such staff have, accordingly, expanded apace. The expansion was accompanied by some grumbling over cost. Also, the relatively greater increase in their numbers, when compared with the growth in enrollments and faculty, disturbed the academic staff.

In April 2009, the Center for College Affordability and Productivity reported the results of a study of the expansion in support staff. A summary of the report appeared in *The Chronicle of Higher Education*:

> Colleges have added managers and support personnel at a steady, vigorous clip over the past 20 years, . . . far outpacing the growth in student enrollment and instructors. Support staff . . . nearly doubled from 1987 to 2007. Meanwhile, jobs for instructors increased by . . . about 50 percent. Enrollments also grew over this period, but the rate of growth of managers and support staff, many of whose positions did

not exist 20 years ago, increased much faster. The ratio of this group to students rose by 34 percent, compared with just a 10-percent rise in the ratio of instructors to students. . . . [M]ost of the increase in the back-office work force came among support personnel. . . . They include a wide diversity of positions that support the college's academic, student, and institutional operations, like lawyers, librarians, clergy, coaches, and student counselors. Colleges added nearly 300,000 such jobs over the 20-year period, as well as about 64,000 administrators and managers. Academic institutions actually added more instructors, about 625,000, than in the managerial and support categories combined. But most of the new faculty positions were part time. The center's finding that jobs for instructors rose by 50 percent reflects both full-time positions and part-time jobs expressed as full-time equivalents.[1]

An economic downturn, such as was experienced in 2008–2009, concentrates the mind of academic leaders on cost containment, and, most especially, on areas farther from the mind and heart than teaching and research. The magnitude of the issue, especially for leading private and public universities and colleges, is indicated in Table 8-1. It shows the number of FTE (full time equivalent) employees per 100 students in 2007, and the increase in the ratio of FTE employees to students in the decade from 1997–2007, for twenty universities (10 private and 10 public):

These observations come to mind: (1) the number of FTE staff per 100 students is markedly lower at public universities than it is at private ones; (2) the degree of variation between the university with the largest number of FTE staff per 100 students and the one with the lowest is much greater at the private universities (64 compared to 31) and (25 to 17); and (3) the degree of variation in the ratio increases from 1997 to 2007 and is wide in both types of institution. These variations suggest that there are significant potential savings available to academic leaders. Of course, that conclusion assumes that the needs for support staff are reasonably comparable at the institutions noted (a rather large assumption).

Table 8-1

Institutions with the Largest Ratios of Managerial and Support Workers to Students in 2007

Private Universities	FTE Employees per 100 Students in 2007	Increase in Ratio 1997-2007 (%)
Vanderbilt	64	97
California Inst. of Technology	57	26
Duke	55	3
Univ. of Rochester	40	77
Washington Univ. (St. Louis)	35	35
Yale	35	37
Columbia	34	82
Gallaudet Univ.	34	93
Emory	34	62
Johns Hopkins	31	111

Public Universities	FTE Employees per 100 Students in 2007	Increase in Ratio 1997-2007 (%)
Univ. of Illinois (Chicago)	25	40
New Mexico Inst. of Mining & Tech.	20	43
Univ. of Alabama (Birmingham)	25	31
Univ. of Washington (St. Louis)	24	45
Univ. of Michigan (Ann Arbor)	20	13
Univ. of Pittsburgh (Main Campus)	19	60
Univ. of California (San Diego)	19	37
Univ. of California (Los Angeles)	19	51
Georgia Inst. of Technology	19	2
Univ. of Wisconsin (Madison)	17	14

B. Using University Support Functions as a Laboratory for Students

The expansion of support functions provides a laboratory for students. They provide a low-cost asset that can be usefully assigned to assist in the activities of the service departments. For example, business and engineering students can work on institution-related process improvement projects, under the supervision of faculty members, reducing costs or increasing revenues as part of their formal education. This is commonly done at the University of Miami in the School of Business and the College of Engineering. For example, two business students cut the cost of University-owned inventory held on campus from $400,000 to $200,000 per year. The cost was $20,000, for both the student's time and the faculty supervisor's time. This was a win-win-win scenario as students acquired practical experience applying the knowledge they had learned in the classroom; faculty supervisors gained extra compensation; and the university decreased its costs by 10 times its investment in the first year.

C. Outsourcing Service Functions

The management of service functions in an academic institution does not usually require direct, frequent attention by presidents or deans. It is usually overseen by vice presidents. But occasionally, issues arise that do involve the top leadership of the institution. Illustrative of such issues are outsourcing service functions to private business contractors, unionization of those private business contractors, and the quality of services provided. In addition, there are organizational matters that need to be addressed.

Administrators who favor keeping services in-house usually argue that it ensures a higher and more consistent quality, because the university has direct control of the personnel and products used. Those who favor outsourcing argue the opposite because the provider faces competition for the business. One can argue the matter endlessly, but our experience seems to indicate that the latter point of view is likely to be more correct. It seems that in-house arrangements can be associated with an attitude among the employees that they are dealing with a captive group of consumers, and they develop a bureaucratic sense of being secure despite the quality of the service being delivered. We have no data available as to the percent of universities and colleges having one or the other arrangement, or their relative degree of satisfaction.

Ultimately, academic managers must determine whether to perform services in-house, or to outsource them to private business contractors, e.g., dining services to Chartwells, or the book store to Follett. In the latter case, there is a further question: should the outside contractor be unionized or not?

D. Unionization of Outside Contractors

The union issue hardly ruffled the placid surface of academic life in prior periods. In the post-World War II years, the American trade union scene was dominated by powerful industrial and craft unions who saw private industry as their organizational targets. But in recent decades, traditional private sector unions have declined drastically in membership and power, as the industries and trades that they bargained with have diminished as a proportion of the nation's economy. The service sector has gained greatly, as manufacturing employment gave way to competition from emerging industrial powers like the Asian Tigers (Japan, South Korea, Taiwan, China, India, and others), not to mention Mexico and Brazil.

With those changes, service unions—most notably the Service Employees International Union (SEIU)—have expanded exponentially, especially in the public (government) sector. And SEIU has seen universities as desirable, and relatively easy, organizational targets because many faculty and students leap to defend those they perceive as being economically and socially deprived and weak. All too often, they do not recognize any connection between their support of a union and future tuition rates, or faculty salaries and benefits.

Faculty and students are potent allies for a union organizational drive. Even old-line unions, like the United Automobile Workers or the Teamsters Union, perceived the tempting target. They undertook small organizational efforts among university employees, including part-time faculty and graduate assistants. But none of them seemed as well prepared, or as artful and creative in their strategy and tactics, as the SEIU. No doubt this result is testimony to the organizational genius and soaring ambition of the union's former president, Andrew Stern. He showed greater insight into the economic, political, and social realities of contemporary America than many of his peers in the trade union movement.

Perhaps the best recent example of unionization of outsourced service functions within universities is the University of Miami. In 2006–2007, the SEIU began an effort to unionize the janitorial employees of the university. But the university had outsourced that service to a private, non-union contractor that resisted unionization of its workforce. The union claimed that it had signed up a majority of the employees involved, but the employer challenged that assertion, and demanded a secret ballot of the employees to be conducted by the monitors of the National Labor Relations Board. The SEIU was not too confident of winning such a ballot and refused. Consequently, there was a deadlock between the parties.

The union decided to pressure the university to demand acquiescence by the employer. To that end, it organized picket lines at the university and marshaled those faculty and students who were willing, as well as the public press, to disrupt the university's normal routines. In particular, the pressure was aimed at Dr. Donna Shalala, the university's president. Dr. Shalala was a unique target for she had been a prominent cabinet member in President Clinton's administration. She was known as having liberal leanings, and being friendly to labor. But she refused to use any pressure to compel the employer to agree to a voting procedure that sacrificed the workers' right to a secret ballot. In any case, Dr. Shalala and the university eventually succumbed, and the SEIU achieved victory in that contest. Whether that victory portends further union inroads among the workers performing service functions for universities and colleges will be seen only with the passage of time.

E. Some Examples of Service Functions

Some examples of service functions, in no particular order of importance, are offered. They include Campus Security, Campus Sports Facilities (Stadiums, etc.), Information Technology, and Human Resources Management.

1. Environment and Safety

Although campus security is not a relatively large expenditure item for a university or college, it is a very important one in terms of the institution's image. One traumatic incident can bring, beyond its immediate human cost in suffering, longer-term costs in diminution of the school's reputation as a locus of learning and respect for intellectual dialogue.

Two basic approaches are available for managing campus security: reactive management and proactive management. Reactive management is illustrated by Examples 1 and 2 below, excellent case studies of good after-the-fact management. The authors are of the opinion that it is usually better to proactively prevent problems from occurring than to react to them once they have occurred. But we are not prescient and always able to anticipate future tragedies, so there will be, inevitably, incidents which will involve reactive management.

Example 1

A situation that is disruptive of research and instruction involves phoned bomb threats, especially during final exam periods. This sort of thing occurs intermittently, but is most likely during periods of political and social unrest, like the late sixties and early seventies of the twentieth century. America's campuses were riled then with sit-ins and other demonstrations of protest, sometimes violent. What a convenient cover for an unprepared student when the day of a final exam arrives! Simply phone into the dean's office, and announce that a bomb will go off in the building where the exam is scheduled. Some degree of panic ensues, and everyone looks to the presumably omniscient dean to decide whether to evacuate the building. Of course, that disrupts the target exam and requires some arrangement for rescheduling. It also disrupts the business of hundreds of other exam takers, who are diligent and prepared.

What should the dean do? She or he may know from experience that 99.9% of the time the call is a ruse. But suppose this time it isn't. How will the dean explain a decision not to evacuate in that case? In precisely such a moment, a dean can turn to the campus security office and ask: "Is there any reliable indicator by which one can determine whether a bomb threat is real?" The dean at NYU was told there was, but it was kept a secret because only then could one trust it. He was told that real bomb threats always specified the time and location of the explosion, and left only sufficient time for evacuation. At that time (late 1960s), universities were not dealing with bombers who intended to inflict death and injury to as many people as they could. With that knowledge, he ordered that before every final exam period the building be searched by the security department. Following that, students and others arriving for exams were to pass by a check table manned by guards. Anyone with a bag or parcel would have to open same for scrutiny. Having taken those precautions, he ordered that anytime a threat was called in, the secretary was to note and repeat the exact language of the call to him or a trusted colleague. The secretarial staff was not told the reason for taking special note of the language of the call. If the caller did not give the critical information of time and place, then no evacuation was to occur. It was amazing. The epidemic of bomb threats simply ceased. But the dean hoped that if, heaven forbid, a bomb did detonate, it would do so beneath the chair he was occupying. Then he wouldn't have to explain his failure to evacuate the structure.

Example 2

Another interesting episode was the case of the psychotic professor. John S. was a tenured full professor who had been at NYU's School of Commerce for over eighteen years. He had been on a leave of absence to teach in India and Africa. Professor S. had been away for several years, with no evident plans to return. Yet, he occupied a tenured professorial slot at a time when the faculty was undergoing a massive shrinkage in numbers due to a collapse in the school's enrollments. The dean wrote to him, asking when he planned to return. If he had no such intention, his position would be retired. But if he planned to come back, then the cutback would involve another faculty member's leaving.

Professor S. responded affirmatively, and the department chairman scheduled classes for him. In due time, he arrived, and reported for service. Several weeks after the term started, students from his classes came to the dean's office, and reported bizarre behavior. Professor S. had come to class equipped with a camera. He announced to the students that he was aware that there was an international conspiracy against him, led by a Grand Master who intended to kill him. Professor S. continued, saying that he was also aware that a few of the Grand Master's agents were in his classes, and he was taking pictures so that they would know that he was watching them. He would then position his camera on his desk, and appear to actually be taking photos of students.

Imagine the dean's shock as this tale was told. The matter had to be addressed. He considered what specific action to take: at no time during the dean's academic career had anyone provided training for dealing with such a bizarre situation. The reality was that it was the dean's responsibility as the school's leader to make judgments and decisions. He called the university's staff psychiatrist, a fine and experienced physician. He was told that the situation was potentially dangerous and would require that Professor S. be instructed to go immediately to see the doctor. The dean called the professor, whom he knew as a colleague for many years, and asked him to come in. He also removed all items from his desk that might possibly be used as weapons, alerted his office staff to send Professor S. in immediately upon arrival, and arranged for the security office to have appropriate professional staff secreted in a next door office, available if needed.

After those precautions, the professor arrived. The dean greeted him as a long-time colleague and friend. Then, he told the professor that odd stories had come to his attention, and they could not be ignored, even though they didn't seem plausible. Nonetheless, it was necessary for the professor to proceed immediately to the doctor's office and speak to him. Professor S. demurred at first, but the dean told him that if he failed to follow those instructions then higher university authority with less sympathy for the professor would take charge, and the dean would be unable to be of any help. Professor S. did as asked. Following his visit, the psychiatrist called the dean and told him to immediately relieve the professor of his classes and order him to come under the care of a qualified psychiatrist of his choice. The dean put him on sick leave with full pay. A year went by. Professor S. returned with a letter from his psychiatrist saying that he was all right and could resume his teaching.

Once again, he was assigned classes and began the new semester. A few weeks passed, and some of his students appeared in the dean's office, repeating the complaints of the prior year. This time, after consultation with the university psychiatrist, it was decided that the professor could not continue in his position. But he was a tenured full professor, and to fire him for cause could well precipitate a harmful legal situation, as well as precipitate a dangerous crisis with an unstable faculty member. The dean called in the professor, with the precautions of a year earlier repeated. He told Professor S. that matters were now out of his control, and advised the professor to retain an attorney to help negotiate a settlement that would permit the professor to leave without any scandal or negative publicity, thus giving him time to overcome his problems. The professor retained one of America's best-known attorneys, with a reputation as a staunch defender of the underdog. The attorney was William Kunstler, who, after meeting Professor S. and spending some time with him, called the dean, and advised him to settle and remove the

Professor from the scene. A settlement was forthcoming. It was approved by the central administration.

2. Sports Facilities

Generally, Sports Facilities, Information Technology, and Human Resources Management are under the purview of the central administration of the university or college, and will be the responsibility of a vice president, or other equivalent administrator. In that case, students and faculty are customers in the traditional business sense. Their satisfaction is important to the total experience of being part of an intellectual community. If they find themselves ill served and are unhappy, they will in time spread the word that their school is deficient in those essentially nonacademic aspects of student life. Of course, if the institution is a famous academic center, that aura will overcome what may then seem rather petty complaints. Even there, however, students and faculty have choices among several peer schools. So, excellence in all parts of the academic experience is significant. After all, there is an attitudinal aspect to the matter. Good managers are usually attentive to all aspects of an operation, and slack ones are the opposite.

Sports, while seemingly separate and apart from the academic sphere, do have a significant and direct connection to it. For one thing, there is likely to be a physical education department in the school of education, or some other academic unit dedicated to provide instruction in sports management. They will have academic standing and present graduates for university degrees. There is also the management and maintenance of sports facilities such as stadiums, fitness centers, special housing, and academic support facilities. Tension between the academic and sports sides of university life has been discussed at length earlier in this book. Such conflicts generally occur at universities and colleges with Division I sports teams (football and basketball most prominently). They compete fiercely for the most prominent high school athletes, offering scholarships and other inducements (allegedly arranging admission to the university for academically weak students). Once admitted, they will often be directed into specific departments for their academic work, and may even be directed into specific courses with specific professors. Whenever this happens, it is supposed to be surreptitious, but it has a way of eventually being exposed to everyone's embarrassment. In terms of claims on institutional resources, Division I sports programs often involve important and expensive construction of stadiums and other limited-use facilities.

Rutgers University, New Jersey's leading public research university, has suffered some very bad publicity relating to its football program. Rutgers' drive to become a significant Division I football school brought bad consequences, not the least of which involved financial obligations. To lead the effort, Rutgers recruited an expensive football coach with an annual compensation package of over $2 million (together with a secret arrangement allowing the coach to abandon the position without sacrificing a $500,000 penalty specified in the main body of his employment contract). The penalty provision was related to the timely completion of a $102-million enlargement and modernization of the Rutgers football stadium. The stadium project was intended to expand seating by 14,000. It was to be financed by a $30 million fundraising campaign, and borrowing (presumably through the issuance of tax-free bonds) in the amount of $72 million. The fund-raising drive was an abysmal failure, apparently stalling after receipt of only $2 million in pledges. In the meantime, other sports teams (tennis, swimming, and fencing) at Rutgers were downgraded to intramural status to save money for the football program. Other consequences involved an allegedly excessive number of football scholarships, and significant cost overruns on the stadium project.

Reference to stadiums, coupled with other sports-related facilities, reminds us that these expensive and complex additions to university or college plant and equipment, have to be managed and maintained. An especially hazardous financial exposure is involved. The construction of these facilities often is related to donor-pledges. If the pledges are not fulfilled, the university or college is on the hook for the shortfall. The burden can impact the institution's ability to accomplish its academic mission. That outcome, unintended as it is, can be prevented by prudent, competent management.

3. Information Technology: Hackers

The Information Technology (IT) department performs multiple functions. The critical ones are: (1) creating an environment that promotes state-of-the-art learning opportunities and positive educational experiences for faculty and staff who are limited in their knowledge of IT equipment and usage; (2) providing an infrastructure of equipment and support staff necessary to the teaching and learning goals of a research university; (3) facilitating communication between and among providers and users of IT services, so that possible problems are mitigated, and current problems resolved efficiently; (4) advising the institution, and its constituent units, of advances in IT technology; and (5) recommending (planning) relevant budgetary requirements for IT.

There are latent problems and tensions that are easily exacerbated because the several schools and divisions of the university or college usually differ in the degree of IT sophistication possessed by faculty and staff. For example, the Computer Science or Mathematics faculties may have very different IT needs than the faculties in Sociology, Philosophy, or History. Further, there is a potential organizational problem associated with the IT structure of the university or college, that is: are there separate IT service departments, or is there only a central office? If a combination exists, then their interactions are important and need to be managed.

At NYU in the late 1970s, there was a basic issue relating to the type of equipment configuration that should be developed by the university. It was a time when individual desktop computers were becoming increasingly powerful, making possible a decentralized and interactive configuration between desktops and a central database. The alternative was a large-capacity mainframe that would be a central information computing resource, to which other divisions of the university would turn for computing and information needs.

The issue was resolved by a university-wide committee, headed by the then dean of the School of Commerce, and composed of representatives from the several schools and colleges. One of its most influential members was a senior faculty member from the Courant Institute of Mathematical Science. Given his technical knowledge of prospective developments in the IT field, the committee recommended the decentralized configuration. Today, the age of dominant mainframes for most applications has been succeeded by individual laptops that are ubiquitous and possessed by almost all members of the university or college community. Of course, contemporary laptops have information and computing power beyond the capacity of the mainframes of four decades ago. In that case, the committee's approach to resolving a basic organizational issue worked well. More recently, computers capable of handling massive amounts of data have altered the appropriate configuration of equipment.

Today, IT confronts America's research universities and colleges with a more profound threat to their core academic mission: the openness that is fundamental to free research and intellectual interaction. The threat arises from the multitude of efforts by hackers world-wide to break into the computer systems of academic institutions. These attacks often originate in China and Russia (with or without government involvement), with the intention of stealing and then selling valuable information. The University of Wisconsin (Madison) reports an amazing, even incredible, volume of such attempts to breach its computer systems: 90,000 efforts per day. Purdue University and others have also reported break-in attempts.[2] Anti-hacker defense is expensive, but vital. Yet, it is not commonly thought about as a significant problem for university administrators.

4. Human Resources (Nonacademic Staff)

Efficient human resource management minimizes the risk to the university from incompetent or negligent faculty, staff, and/or administrators. Usually, human resource management in universities and colleges encompasses the following functions: (1) recruiting, selecting, and hiring; (2) professional training and career development; (3) succession planning; (4) performance evaluation, promotions, demotions and terminations; (5) employee relations and union negotiations, where relevant; (6) compensation and benefits planning (including pension and health); and (7) records maintenance.

Human resource management in universities and colleges does not perform the first four functions. The reason is the diffuse governmental tradition of academic institutions. Tenure-track faculty members handle those functions. Of course, their decisions are subject to review by deans and university provosts (or other agents of the president), but any administrator who treats faculty recommendations cavalierly runs the serious and consequential risk of a hue and cry that can shorten his or her tenure.

It should occasion no surprise that tenure-track faculty usually lack expertise in human resource management, and probably look askance at any suggestions that industrial relations models might be applicable to academic institutions. After all, they are scholars. They study and do research to obtain the doctorate, the highest and most difficult academic degree. Nothing in their education as scholars is designed to produce professional managers (unless they have acquired a business school degree along the way). Since academic administrators are drawn from the ranks of the faculty, it is understandable that they learn the other skills on the job, or later in life, when they realize that they need specific, nonacademic tools and skills to administer academic organizations. However, wise academic administrators will use professional human resource managers to perform the functions noted above for nonacademic staff and administrators.

Notes

1. *The Chronicle of Higher Education*, April 24, 2009, A1, A16–A18.
2. Richard Perez-Pena, "Campuses Face Rising Threat From Hackers," *The New York Times*, July 17, 2013, A1, A15.

Chapter 9

The University President: The Leader's Job is Critical

A. The University or College President

In Chapter 2, we called the university or college president the institution's chief executive officer. We did not call him its chief academic officer, although she or he is both. The choice of terminology reflects a prolonged and persistent shift in the nature of the position. Traditionally, the institution's president was perceived as an academic, a scholar focused on knowledge and its transmission, as well as extension and encouragement of critical thinking. S/he was not perceived primarily as an executive; a "boss" focused on the management of the institution and its financial health. Yet, today the executive aspect of the position has become dominant.

A 2013 survey of 400 presidents and chancellors of four year colleges revealed that finance had become their major concern, and that fundraising and budgets consumed more than half of their daily work. The survey stated: "Although college presidents preside over academic and research enterprises, their jobs have become more like those of corporate CEOs in recent decades, more directly focused on raising money, balancing budgets, and directing strategy."[1] The academic side of the president's position is now commonly made the responsibility of a chancellor or provost.

College and university presidents, according to the 2013 survey, are older white men (87 percent are white, 78 percent are men, and 61 percent are 60 and older). Given that 3 in 5 presidents are in their 60s, it's likely that the president's office will see turnover in the near future. This likelihood is strengthened by the fact that almost 25 percent of the presidents responding to the survey have been in the job for 10 years or longer. Increasingly, presidents are promoted from within the institution; from 19 percent in a 2005 survey to 25 percent in 2013. In this respect, the presidency is also becoming more business-like. For decades, corporate America has promoted executives from within the organization to the CEO position. Also, academic deans are more likely to move directly into a presidency than before; today, one in ten college presidents came from the dean's office. In terms of preparedness for the president's job, of incumbents who were promoted from the provost's or chief academic officer's position, 50 percent reported that they were extremely well prepared for the president's job. Of those promoted from a non-academic VP or similar position, 53 percent reported that they were extremely well prepared. When asked to rank 18 measures of success for their presidencies, the number 1 indicator was a balanced budget. Strengthening the institution's reputation was next, but the presidents did not accept *The US News & World Report* rankings as a true indicator. Indeed, it was "dead" last among the indicators in the survey. The measures of institutional quality most favored were rates of placement in graduate/professional education, job placement rates, and graduation rates. The least favored were peer assessment/reputation surveys and rankings, e.g., *US News & World Report.*

When it comes to the value of higher education, presidents are more optimistic than employers are. According to the survey, 82 percent of the presidents believed higher education was doing an excellent or good job of providing academic programs that meet the needs of today's economy. A separate survey of employers looking to hire recent college graduates, done by *The Chronicle of Higher Education* in 2012, reported that it was very difficult or difficult to find qualified workers for jobs (slightly over 50 percent). Viewed from another angle, 73 percent of presidents said their students were either well prepared or very well prepared for the job market upon graduation, while only 20 percent of employers said the same about recent college graduates. Although strongly supportive of internships and experiential learning, presidents favored academic credentials over experience as an indicator of recent graduates success in getting jobs after graduation. Employers, on the other hand, favored experience.

The sharply different views of presidents and employers as to the post-graduation employability of university and college students implies a profound difference of perception as to the value of their education. That perceptual difference reflects an underlying difference in the criteria applied by presidents and employers in making their respective judgments as to employability. Employers are concerned about first-job employability, while presidents (and academics generally) are concerned about achieving the aims of the academic mission (transmission of knowledge, extension of knowledge, and development of critical thinking). The latter aims are concerned with preparing students for intelligent participation as citizens of a free society, while the former are narrowly focused on the skills required to perform specific types of jobs (accounting, law, medicine, management, engineering, science, i.e., chemistry, physics, biology, etc.). In today's world, the conflict is joined in the humanities, which seems to some almost irrelevant to jobs and employability.

Some have objected strenuously to this view of the humanities as dead or dying. They observe that, although the humanities as a share of all undergraduate majors has declined sharply from the almost 40% several decades ago, it has been stable at a little less than 8% for many years. It has risen in some years, but not to over 10%. These staunch supporters of the humanities observe further that the humanities have particular importance intellectually to Academe's central mission of developing critical thinking. It is relevant to note that humanities majors, while they do not earn as much as those trained for immediate employability after graduation, earn more generally in later life, when analytical ability becomes more critical in higher level and executive positions. This insight explains why college presidents consider a broad undergraduate education a better preparation for life than those focused on first-job employability.

The difference in viewpoint is sharply reflected when one contrasts the opinions of presidents of four year *private* non-profit colleges with those of for-profit institutions. Of the former group, 72% said the primary mission of their institutions was promoting intellectual and personal growth; 25% said employability. In the case of presidents of four year *public* not-for-profit colleges, 71% said promoting intellectual and personal growth; while 28% said employability. When one turns to the presidents of *for-profit* institutions, however, the picture is overwhelmingly reversed; only 15% said intellectual and personal growth, while a whopping 85% said employability.[2] A resolution is needed; one which appreciates the value of generalists as well as specialists. The burden of responsibility rests primarily on the leaders and faculty of universities and colleges.

That burden of responsibility brings us to the governance of academic institutions. Faculty share in governance, being involved in matters relating to curriculum, tenure, hiring and firing of academic staff, research, and teaching. All are related, in greater or lesser degree, to academic mission, and its marriage to employability. Since our universities embrace a host of professional schools, as well as the Arts & Sciences, (the traditional home of the humanities), there is a difference in faculty views of institutional mission that parallels that between presidents and employers. Of course, there is some overlap between the views of the faculties of Arts & Sciences and the professional schools. While the overlap provides a wedge opening towards reconciliation, it does not, by itself, achieve it. The problem of achieving a reconciliation of the differences lies with the faculties and president. But the initiative rests primarily on the president. Unfortunately, the current focus of presidents on financial and budgetary matters lessens their attention to matters of institutional mission. What is probably needed is an understanding and appreciation of both areas of higher education. It is the burden of leadership to muster and lead the faculty to the marriage ceremony. It is also the burden of leadership to explain to employers the nature of the problem, and their responsibility to be part of its resolution. The exercise of that leadership goes to the heart of the governance problem. Because presidents are consumed now with budgets and finance, while faculty have less interest in those matters, reconciliation is made more difficult. An outcome of this lack of interest is an expansion of administrative authority; which grows at the expense of shared governance. The growth in the executive-management aspect of the presidency manifests itself in more frequent complaints, by faculty, of overreaching authority and unilateral decision-making by presidents and their administrative agents, e.g., vice-presidents. Serious organizational disharmony and mischief results. Appreciation of the problem precedes any resolution. And, a resolution rests inevitably on an exercise of leadership by university and college presidents.

B. Achieving and Leaving Leadership in the Academy: Stepping Up and Stepping Down

At a number of points in our exploration of the challenges that confront administrative leadership in universities and colleges, we discussed the qualities and characteristics (the aptitudes and attitudes) that contribute to success in the key positions of president and dean. We have not considered, to this point, the paths that lead to those positions of leadership and responsibility. We now undertake to fill that gap.

1. Stepping Up

a. The Search Committee

It has become common practice when a university or college presidency, or a deanship, is to be filled, to appoint a search committee. In the case of a presidency, the committee will probably be appointed by the board of trustees, and may include trustee representation. Depending upon the traditions and particular practices of the university or college, there will be significant representation from the faculty and deans. There may also be a representative of the student body, usually selected from the institution's student government leadership. The wise student, in that case, observes, thinks much, and says little, while learning a great deal about the psychological dynamics of committee behavior, as well as about institutional governance. The brash student, on the other hand, hardly observes, being consumed by a perception of self-importance, thinks little, and says much, becoming quickly marginalized, while learning almost nothing. The chairmanship of the committee will frequently be filled by another dean or a prominent faculty member, who is well regarded internally and externally. There will probably be some staff available to the committee, to handle records (agendas, minutes), meeting and interview schedules, and budgets, among other things.

Once constituted, the committee must organize itself, and decide several matters listed here, not necessarily in order of importance: (1) the qualities sought in prospective candidates; (2) the compensation and benefits associated with the position (tenure and professorial status, salary, pension and medical care, housing, expenses for travel and other activities, car and driver); (3) other relevant institutional data to be provided to candidates; (4) avenues to be used in publicizing the position (*The Chronicle of Higher Education*, The AAUP magazine, *Academe*, leading national newspapers, professional scholarly journals, and so on); (5) the services of a leading "head hunter" firm; and (6) the conduct of candidate interviews, as well as the vetting of those candidates who seem most promising.

A relevant example is provided by Florida International University (FIU) in Miami.[3] The *Miami Herald* described the activities of the search committee appointed by the university's trustees to find a new president to replace President Modesto Maidique (who was stepping down after almost 23 years of service that brought the institution to an enrollment of 38,000 students, with robust graduate programs). While FIU is not among America's major research universities, it is clearly a "want-to-be," with large ambitions that include a newly state-approved medical school. The presidential search committee indicated that its new president would likely be offered a compensation package worth as much as $680,000, about $50,000 more than the current president's. This figure was reached following a report to the board of trustees by a commission which had studied presidential compensation packages at comparable universities, the school announced that eighteen candidates had expressed interest in the job, including presidents, deans and provosts from other institutions. The compensation package included a $500,000 base salary and $180,000 in such perks as deferred compensation, signing and retention bonuses, housing allowance, and moving cost. The commission's study took into account the income of the presidents of twenty-two institutions comparable to FIU.

The trustees finally whittled the number of candidates from eighteen to three. Two were FIU insiders (the current provost and a professor who had served as an FIU dean, as well as Chancellor of the Florida State University System), while the third was an outsider, who was serving as chancellor of the University of Wisconsin at Milwaukee. Shortly before the FIU board of trustees met to decide which candidate would be their choice, two of the candidates withdrew (the outsider and the current FIU provost, who announced his acceptance of the position of chancellor of Cleveland State University). The remaining candidate, Professor Mark Rosenberg, was then formally announced as the board's choice. The outcome suggests that the process, in this case, was weighted in favor of one of the internal candidates, but we do not know whether that is the fact. It is always possible that a particularly strong and attractive outside candidate would have gained the committee's and the board's approval, and emerged as the choice.[4] In any case, the *Miami Herald's* report noted: "Rosenberg's naming was not totally free of controversy. Some of the other candidate's supporters felt his candidacy was treated unfairly by internal Rosenberg supporters. And some wondered if the job was Rosenberg's all along."

b. The Qualities Sought in Prospective Candidates

Surely, one of the most critical tasks before the committee is to determine and articulate the most important qualities (attributes) wanted in a candidate. While the *Herald* story of the FIU search committee fails to discuss the qualities that the search committee sought in candidates, it did imply an understanding of the "talent" wanted. What are the talents wanted in presidents, as well as deans and provosts, in universities and colleges, including those that aspire to advance in academic prestige?

Before describing those talents, we are impelled to observe that institutions aspiring to achieve prominence in Division I sports will manifest greater readiness to pay outsize compensation packages to top coaches than they do to their presidents. A prime example is provided by basketball coach John Calipari, who moved from the University of Memphis to the University of Kentucky, after being offered an eight-year contract worth $31.65 million, and thereby becoming the highest paid coach in college basketball. A report in *The New York Times* describing the offer and its context, noted that it was strongly supported by the president (Dr. Lee T. Todd, Jr.) and the Athletic Director (Mitch Barnhart) of the University of Kentucky. Barnhart said, "We're the pre-eminent basketball program in the country and if we want a premier coach, then that may be what it takes to get it done.[5]

For lesser luminaries, like university and college presidents, provosts, and deans, who are presumably focused on the academic mission of their institutions, the following qualities seem to us to be necessary: (1) vision of a mission and strategy for the institution, as well as the type of faculty and students sought, the nature of the curriculum, and so forth; (2) a concept of management suitable to the culture of a university or college, coupled with comprehension of such matters as budgets, organizational structure, and administration; (3) an understanding of the values that are critical in a community of scholars (freedom of inquiry and expression, the importance of evidence and striving for consensus); (4) an understanding, in the absence of consensus, of the necessity for courage and determination in making and implementing hard and painful decisions (most particularly in a context of academic paradigm shift or financial crisis); (5) acceptance of the necessity for fundraising, and, even when finding it distasteful, readiness to perform in that role; (6) possession of the communication and social skills needed to win the support of important constituencies; and (7) of particular importance, but difficult to ascertain, the ability to respond quickly and effectively to unexpected and apparently random events. We will say more of this below. Such a combination of aptitudes may be a great deal to ask for, especially when it involves a mix of scholarly sensibilities and pragmatism. Nonetheless, that combination is what it can take to do an outstanding job.

c. The Interview

The search committee will organize itself, and establish a timetable for the completion of its task. Initially, it must decide the matters discussed above, i.e., the qualities sought in candidates, the data that must be gathered relative to compensation and other conditions, the vitae of prospective candidates, the number of candidates to be finally submitted to the board of trustees, in the case of the presidency, or to the president, in the case of a deanship (for his/her recommendation to the board), the number of interviews to be scheduled in the search for the final candidates or candidate, and other such relevant material.

The interview should not be seen by members of the committee as a one-way process, in which the meeting is solely designed to evaluate the candidate. Equally important, in terms of successful outcomes, is the fact that the candidate is assessing the university or college, especially when she or he is being recruited from another institution. The committee can expect that candidates have devoted some pre-interview time and thought to the institution they are considering, and should inquire into candidates' perceptions about the position and the conditions associated with it. There should be candor in the exchange of information by both parties. So called "snow jobs" will likely result in disappointment and problems after a candidate's appointment is approved. Interviews should not be rushed; the parties are not negotiating a commercial transaction of physical commodities. Usually, time will be provided for some social interaction between some or all members of the search committee and the candidate, perhaps over lunch or dinner. And the interview visit should allow time for the candidate to see the campus—its academic facilities, as well as housing, recreational, and other amenities. In the case of a presidency, the interview process will perforce involve meetings with trustees. It may also involve a meeting with the incumbent president, although this would probably be dependent on the circumstances associated with her or his retirement or resignation. In the case of a deanship, the candidate should certainly meet the president. Once again, a meeting with the incumbent dean would probably be dependent on the circumstances associated with her or his departure. No matter what the arrangements made by the search committee, there may be informal contacts by both parties in their respective pursuit of information.

Everything described so far is intended to enhance and make more likely the achievement of a successful relationship, that is, to make such an outcome more predictable. But there is a significant element of chance involved. All involved are no doubt on their best behavior, and the most appealing candidate can turn out to be quite different from what she or he seemed during the interview. By the same token, aspects of the leadership position may turn out to be quite different from what was represented. For example, a university or college seeking to achieve an academic paradigm shift during a period of general prosperity and very successful fundraising may make commitments to a candidate that cannot be fully, or even partially, fulfilled in the face of a sudden national financial crisis (such as was experienced in 2008–2009). Such a situation suggests that the most important characteristic in a candidate may be the ability to react decisively in providing leadership during an unexpected and random change in circumstances.

Nassin Nicholas Taleb's book, *The Black Swan,* comes to mind.[6] Taleb observed that prior to the discovery of Australia, Europeans were firmly convinced that all swans were white. The belief was based on the empirical evidence of millennia, because all swans in Europe were in fact white. But then, Australia was discovered, and in that distant land there were black swans. Taleb notes that this experience

> illustrates a severe limitation to our learning from observations or experience. . . . One single observation can invalidate a general statement derived from millennia" [of observation and experience]. . . . What we call here a Black Swan (and capitalize it) is an event with the following three attributes. First, it is an *outlier*, as it lies outside the realm of regular expectations, because nothing in the past can convincingly point to its possibility. Second, it carries an extreme impact. Third, in spite of its outlier status, human nature makes us concoct

explanations for its occurrence *after* the fact, making it explainable and predictable. . . . It is easy to see that life is the cumulative effect of a handful of significant shocks. How often do things occur according to plan?

We do not cite Taleb's Black Swan to decry planning which, in fact, does enable one to deal with the ordinary and usually repetitive realities of life. Probability is a useful concept, even though it does not and cannot predict Black Swans. We cite it to point up the significance of an ability in administrators to deal with an unexpected and unpredictable turn of events. We seek to emphasize also the poor payout one gets from the tendency, when confronted by an unexpected and adverse event, to look backward and find others to blame for the consequences. What really counts under such circumstances is the ability to look ahead, and deal decisively with the problems that can threaten the survival of an institution or organization. That is the most critical quality one should seek in a leader, whether in Academe or elsewhere.

d. Paths to a Top Leadership Position in a University or College

Path 1. The Tap on the Shoulder

This is one of at least three such paths. One of the authors was unaware that his name was put forward to become dean by a colleague, who was a member of a search committee seeking to fill that position. He became aware only after the committee decided to nominate him, and he was invited to see an executive dean who was acting as an agent of the university president. With the positive recommendation of that administrator, he was then invited to an interview with the president. As an interesting sidelight, we note that the position was dean of a business school that was in a financial, enrollment, and curricular, i.e., academic, crisis. In fact, the school faced a trustee and presidential mandate to make a paradigm-shifting academic transformation, and to make it quickly, or to face termination. The president had forced the retirement of the previous dean, who resisted the demanded change, and who, quite frankly, hadn't a clue as to what was necessary.

The president was seeking a person who struck him as being a scholar, who had a broad liberal arts orientation, and was an advocate of a solid general education as the basis for the professional education that then was offered by the school. The interview was an extraordinary experience. The dean candidate expected to be asked about his views on such matters as mission, strategy, curriculum, and faculty credentials. Instead, the president, who had examined the nominee's vitae and undoubtedly noted that he was a professor of economics, was evidently surprised at the title of his doctoral dissertation: "The Economics of the Mt. Hagen Tribes of New Guinea," which was published by J. J. Augustin and sponsored by the American Ethnological Society. Without any lengthy explanation, it will have to suffice to note that the topic was an outcome of need by an ABD (All But Dissertation) doctoral candidate at Columbia University. A series of lucky, propitious coincidences had put the candidate in New Guinea during World War II as Assistant Historical Officer of the Far East Air Service Command. This position gave him access to Father William A. Ross, a missionary of the Society of the Divine Word, who had established a pioneering mission station at Mt. Hagen just prior to the war. The university president and the prospective dean spent the entire interview discussing New Guinea, and Cargo Cults, a postwar development among the then primitive natives in the inner highlands of New Guinea. The president never raised any question about the business school, and decided that such an apparently odd person was exactly the one he wanted to lead the School of Commerce. We can call such a path to a deanship as being a "Tap on the Shoulder."

It is probably appropriate to note additionally that the faculty colleague who was a member of the search committee, and who nominated the dean-to-be, had himself been asked by the executive dean if he were interested in being put forward for the position, and had turned it down. His nominee, however, only learned that fact some forty-three years later, when both men were very senior citizens (ages 90 and 96). Of course, the former nominee was most curious about the reason. He was told that his "sponsor" (who was then a department head) knew that highly unpleasant decisions would be required of the successful nominee, had felt that he, himself, could not implement such decisions and be emotionally at peace. However, he believed that his nominee, while he might not be happy over what needed to be done, would have the stomach to make decisions that would be very painful to more than a few colleagues (an expectation that turned out to be accurate).

Another noteworthy facet of the "Tap on the Shoulder" path to academic leadership, especially in the case of deans, is that, at least initially, it can be a source of decision-making power. Not having sought the position, the new dean probably has no initial intrinsic, emotional need to hang onto it. She or he is not yet "in love" with the title and the social and economic opportunities that it can present (board directorships, which can be quite remunerative, and invitations from prominent and wealthy alumni to visit their homes in pleasant and interesting places, e.g., Marrakesh, Majorca, Barbados, and so on). Of course, the latter invitations can be used for effective fundraising purposes. Having little or no fear of surrendering the position, readiness to resign if thwarted in implementing painful but necessary decisions, presents the president and the members of the search committee with the somewhat embarrassing need to explain the reason for such a "resignation." And, when the issue is the exercise of strong leadership as against the opposition of fearful and indecisive administrators and faculty who seek to temporize and delay, the president and trustees who approved the appointment are likely to opt for strength.

There is a critical caveat. The resignation offer must not seem like a "temper tantrum." It should be made regretfully and courteously, with quiet firmness, as an issue of organizational necessity required to affect a paradigm shift, or to meet a financial crisis. And it must never be a bluff; if "called," the resignation must follow or all credibility will be lost. But if the opposition "backs down," which our experience indicates is likely under conditions of crisis, then credibility is gained. And once gained, it has importance in the future, whenever those opposing needed changes weigh the likely outcome of a confrontation.

Path 2. Positive Action by the Aspirant

Another path to a leadership position requires positive initiative by the one aspiring to the position. In this case, we have a person who wants the position, and who arranges her/his nomination by finding a colleague or other well-placed intermediary to suggest her or him as a good candidate. An exercise of political skill can be a key element in this case. Some forty-seven years ago, one of the authors witnessed just such an exercise. The then dean, who had been ill for some time, finally decided to retire. The school's associate dean, who had been on the faculty for many years, and had been in the administration for a good part of that time, hungered for the top position. The retiring dean had assumed the position of dean after being recruited from outside the school. In an interim period, the associate dean had served briefly as an acting dean.

But he was then passed over for the leadership position, being judged as wanting in important qualities. However, his hunger for the deanship did not desert him.

Seeing the new opportunity presented, and knowing that he had been passed over before, he decided that he needed a petition from the faculty to put him in the running. To that end, he enlisted a close faculty friend to draft a petition of support, and carry it around seeking faculty signatures. His "lackey," to put the matter unkindly, was energetic in his pursuit of the needed signatures, suggesting to those who hesitated to sign that there would be unpleasant retaliation later. One of the authors, who was a witness, admits somewhat shamefacedly that he signed, doing so with some reluctance, but the belief that deans came and went, and were largely powerless to do any real harm. He learned later how naïve and wrong he was. But there was one faculty member who refused to sign, after telling the would-be dean's agent that he thought the man was not competent. That professor was one of the best known members of the faculty, an outstanding researcher and author of many publications. The outcome was interesting and informative. The associate dean became dean, based on the petition, and proved totally incompetent to handle the enrollment, financial, and academic crises that the school faced. After three years, the university president forced his resignation and retirement. The new dean was the one described above as having received a "Tap on the Shoulder."

Arranging one's own nomination, where there is a search committee, would involve getting a member of the committee to place the candidate's name before the committee. In that case, disclosure of the candidate's availability would be at the discretion of the committee member who actually put the nomination before the committee. Success would then probably hinge on the assessment by the committee of the candidate's qualifications and suitability, unless the committee was somehow influenced by other considerations. Hopefully, that would not be the case. Another path would involve the intermediation of a professional "head hunting" firm. That may be growing in popularity, as search committees seek to use such firms as a convenient and useful screening resource. Another intermediary is also possible, i.e., a colleague, or other person with influential connections, who places the candidate into consideration through another party who is involved in the search or has access to people who are, especially when the position is at a a school other than the candidate's own.

Path 3. Open Solicitation

This path generally involves a search committee. In this case, a candidate can respond to an advertisement of the position. This path has become more widespread since regulations and policies requiring non-discrimination have become prevalent. The need for universities or colleges to demonstrate openness to minorities is somewhat satisfied by an apparent showing of the position's availability, accompanied by statements assuring prospective candidates of that openness. We have no idea how successful this path is, having no data that would prove its effectiveness, or lack thereof. But we do have a suspicion that, when there is an in-house candidate who is highly qualified and well regarded, the outcome will favor that candidate.

2. Stepping Down

Having been appointed to the leadership position of president or dean, and having served in that leadership role for a lengthy (or for a relatively brief time), how does one step down? Is it a voluntary or an involuntary separation? Is it attended with evidences of service well performed, or something quite different? Is there a good or a bad "taste" on the part of the university or college, or on the part of the departing leader? Some comments relevant to these questions are appropriate.

a. Voluntary Departure

A voluntary departure is a decision initiated by a president or dean who decides to step down from her or his position. Such a decision is usually announced as a "resignation" or a "retirement." These are the usual reasons for voluntary departures: (1) age and/or health; (2) family and/or other personal reasons; (3) a desire for new challenges and/or new geographical location; (4) a more important leadership position, with better compensation and perks; (5) dissatisfaction with the current position; or (6) anticipation of a request for one's resignation or retirement, so that one has the satisfaction of keeping the initiative.

Whatever the reason for stepping down, it is always made with the knowledge that academic tenure does not cover administrative appointments, although there may be contractual separation obligations on the part of the institution and/or the administrator. But when the administrator is also a tenured professor, then she or he can leave the administrative position and simply return to the professorial role.

Since mandatory retirement policies are no longer legal (in view of age discrimination provisions of federal law), an administrator who continues in office as a president or dean beyond the age of 65 or 70 does so because she or he is strongly wanted, and strongly desires to continue. But it is our impression that this is unusual. Departures because of health problems need no further explanation, except that sometimes this reason may be given to cover other less agreeable and more contentious ones. Family reasons embrace a host of considerations, e.g., the health of a spouse who needs to relocate to a better climate, or the break-up of a marriage which inclines one to relocate, or getting married, which also can stimulate a move, or children who have special needs that make a move desirable. An administrator may become tired of the position occupied, perhaps because it has become a routine, and lacks new challenges that excite and stimulate. There are people who need such motivations to thrive, and miss them when they are no longer found in the current position. While there are administrators who "fall in love" with their current position and will turn down offers to move up, even when offered superior compensation and perks, many do respond to the lure. Indeed, they are the people who become candidates for stepping up.

Those who do not "fall in love" with their current position may have become disenchanted for a variety of reasons, e.g., policy disputes with the board of trustees, active and organized disaffection among the faculty (Lawrence Summers at Harvard), unhappiness with pressure to be more active in fundraising, or pressure to make and implement difficult decisions under conditions of financial stress. In the case of deans, there may also be disagreements with the central administration over school mission, budgets, faculty promotion and tenure, and so on.

Voluntary departure can be pleasant or unpleasant, depending on the reasons for the separation, and the party who initiated the resignation or retirement. Absent any rancor and coming with mutual agreement that it is a timely and appropriate step, the change in leadership is accompanied by signs and symbols of regard. But these benefits can be nullified if the departing leader discovers that she or he misses the job, or doesn't like the decisions being made by a successor. That situation can become thorny, especially when the ex-dean or president has retired to a position as a tenured full professor. Hanging around and grousing about changes from earlier policies and decisions can poison the well of faculty collegiality. So it is vital that an ex-leader understand the importance of interference only when invited. If that is the behavior pattern followed, then the former administrator may have the satisfaction of becoming a senior counselor whose advice is sought and treasured. What a wonderful way to end a happy life as an academic! Unfortunately, there will be others, perhaps in larger numbers, who become bitter as they perceive that they have become some kind of nonperson.

b. Involuntary Departure

Involuntary termination involves a discharge that reflects dissatisfaction with the performance, or possibly the personality, of a president or dean. In this case, we are concerned with an unpleasant termination, i.e., one that is not covered up by some mutual agreement that attributes it to some other palatable reason. Dissatisfaction with performance can involve incompetence in the leadership role, perhaps in rash or otherwise damaging decisions that prove costly, either financially or in terms of the institution's academic stature. Personality problems can arise from the managerial style of the leader, resulting in faculty disaffection or unhappiness or opposition from among the deans. Or, in the case of the president, there may be a falling out with the board of trustees, although this is probably an unusual situation.

The separation is not necessarily a disaster from the standpoint of the person who is forced to step down. In the case of Lawrence Summers at Harvard, he left the presidency and returned to the faculty as a prestigious professor. In the next couple of years, he is reported to have earned over $7 million as a consultant and invited speaker to groups anxious to have his thoughts on important issues. For a time, he functioned as President Barack Obama's leading adviser on economic issues. Retrospectively, there may be some further thought on the nature of his departure, and who suffered the greater consequent loss. A politically correct decision may not have yielded as much from Professor Summers as he was capable of giving, despite his provocative opinions and alleged managerial toughness in expression and decisions. In the instance of lesser luminaries, an involuntary termination is regarded as a sign of failure, and a bad mark on one's resume.

c. The Interim Appointment

When a presidency or deanship ends unexpectedly, as a consequence of a scandal or a health-related disability, an interim appointment will fill the position, pending the outcome of a search committee's work. A vacancy resulting from a health or other innocent cause can normally be filled temporarily from within the institution. But a vacancy resulting from a scandal requires more draconian measures, i.e., an outside appointment who is unlikely to be tainted by the scandal's aftermath. In that case, what is wanted is someone with experience in a leadership role, who is able to move in, command respect immediately based on an established track record, and be ready to make decisions necessary to overcome the effects of the scandal. A primary consideration in an interim appointment is a clear understanding, in the case of a presidency, between the appointee and the board about the proper role of the board, so that the interim president has real power to act. Such an understanding should avert a situation in which the board chairman, or strong individual board members, interfere in daily operations and/or major operating decisions. An equally clear understanding should be achieved between the president and an interim dean. It is equally important that such understandings should embrace the likely term of the appointment, and especially significant, whether there is any thought of the appointment leading to a permanent position. The temporary nature of the appointment can be a source of strength to the interim appointee, freeing her or him to make unpopular, but necessary, decisions.

Once appointed, the interim leader has to make and implement decisions relative to the normal functions of the position, e.g., curricular, staffing, and fundraising. If the background includes a scandal, then that will probably require immediate and resolute actions: (1) to terminate and replace individuals implicated in the scandal (clean house); and (2) to review and correct any operational procedures or practices that contributed to the scandal. If the institution involved in a scandal is a public university, then the interim president must build a relationship with the governor or other powerful government figures.

C. Peter Magrath, who was appointed as interim president at West Virginia University and who had previously been president of SUNY Binghamton, the University of Minnesota, the University of Missouri system, and the University of Nebraska, described his experience at West Virginia University in a brief article. He accepted the interim presidency after his predecessor resigned, following a scandal involving the daughter of the governor. She had been granted an MBA degree without having properly completed the full credit requirements for the degree. When the situation became public, there was an uproar, and the current president was terminated.

Dr. Magrath, the interim appointee, says that his first order of business was to organize a search committee, working with the chairman of the university's board, to find a new president. Equally important was correcting the operational defects that made the scandal possible, so that a sense of normalcy could be established, and the important work of the institution could go forward. At WVU, sports is an important part of the institution's life, and Dr. Magrath observes: "I would also need to ensure that the intercollegiate athletics program—a big item at the university—was stable and insulated from the political problems so often typical in big-time, Division I sports." He added that, sooner or later, an interim leader would be "tested," and the test would reveal her or his strength of character and leadership ability. In his words:

> My "test" came soon in my brief tenure, not surprisingly in the often treacherous areas of intercollegiate athletics. Thanks to my previous experiences as a president and my strong position as an interim, the university weathered the challenge. I had been pushed to allow a major athletics facility to move forward before all the financial support was in place and to agree that its use would not be fully under university control. I refused.[7]

Needless to say, when Dr. Magrath left WVU, it was with a sense of satisfaction.

Notes

1. Jeffrey J. Selingo, "What President's Think," *The Chronicle of Higher Education*, underwritten by Pearson, 2013, 4 and 6.

2. *The Chronicle of Higher Education, Almanac Issue 2011-2012*, August 26, 2011, 29.

3. *Miami Herald*, April 1, 2009, B1.

4. *Miami Herald*, April 26, 2009, A1-A2.

5. *The New York Times*, April 2, 2009, B13.

6. Nassim Nicholas Taleb, *The Black Swan: The Impact of the Highly Improbable*, (New York: Random House, 2007).

7. *The Chronicle of Higher Education*, February 12, 2010, A80.

Chapter 10

Conclusion

A. The Criteria Underlying Judgment

A re universities and colleges confronted by significant threats to their academic missions? The answer is not susceptible to a categorical *yes or no* response. It depends first, on the criterion applied to judging, i.e., the tripartite academic mission of the institution, as well as the employability mission; and, second, on the *degree* to which the threats faced are fatal to its accomplishment of those missions. We need to recognize at the outset that the ideal is neither 100-percent achievable, nor absolutely necessary to avoid a fatal outcome. Being human and subject to the weaknesses of humankind, there will always be threats that interfere with a complete and absolute ability of the university or college to accomplish the missions. So long as society and its universities and colleges are characterized by freedom, however, teaching need not become indoctrination and research need not be corrupted and distorted. Above all, curiosity and critical thinking must be unfettered and free to roam. In short, the contest will probably be unending. So long as society and the university treasure the ideal, however, the threats should not prove fatal.

B. The Threats Revisited

We will revisit the threats to the university's or college's accomplishment of its academic and employability missions serially, in the order of their discussion in the earlier chapters. We opened with a consideration of the contemporary tumult over the threat posed by online learning and MOOCs. Online learning had been around for some time, being the preferred teaching technology of the for-profit sector of higher education. Its impact had been limited, but it was nonetheless an alternative technology to the traditional, campus based, highly interactive, and interpersonal one of the traditional university. MOOCs, on the other hand, arrived on the scene like a thermonuclear explosion. Coupled with online learning as a necessary handmaiden, it was heralded by some as a revolutionary replacement of the traditional teaching-research technology. Others debated that assessment hotly, maintaining stoutly that it was simply untrue. Of course, the crux of the matter is which methodology is more effective in transmitting and expanding knowledge and, above all, developing critical thinking. Perhaps the proposition should be stated in more absolute terms, i.e., which works and which doesn't? We confess a bias, if it be a bias, in favor of the traditional methodology. Learning and thinking, coupled with mentoring, don't occur *en masse* and online. As a wise sage once observed: education occurs with a teacher on one end of a see-saw and a student on the other end.

Actually, that statement is too rigid. Online learning seems most effective as a teaching technology in certain fields, i.e.. basic science, math, and heavily data-based subject areas. Even there, however, it lacks that mentoring which can be life-long and life-altering. MOOCs are a different matter since some see it as replacing the traditional, interpersonal, and interactive methodology. But once again, that is too rigid a statement. For one thing, there is the issue of course credit toward a bachelor's or graduate degree. There is much debate and considerable faculty resistance toward granting credit for MOOCs although there is some movement in that direction. More important, MOOCs are being altered in the direction of a mixture with traditional methodology, so that they become more attractive to faculty and other critics.

Online learning and MOOCs, in our estimation, are evolutionary, not revolutionary. They will alter, but not replace, the traditional university and college. They will remain to continue their pursuit of the academic and employability missions.

We come now to the deep water of the academic pool. Here we are at the nexus of the institutional missions, where we deal with the authority of administrative appointees, and its being shared and limited by the diffuse power of tenured faculty over curriculum, course content, and academic staff appointments, promotion, tenure, and compensation decisions. Skeptics may sniff at the assertion of faculty power, but the university leader, whether president or provost, dean or vice-president, had better be wary of the ire of an outraged faculty. Those who doubt need only inquire of Larry Summers who resigned Harvard's presidency after some ill-advised comments about women scientists. Or, more recently, ask NYU's president John Sexton who outraged faculty members with his allegedly unilateral decisions to make NYU a global university with fully developed academic clones of the New York institution in Abu Dabai and Shanghai (neither famous for academic freedom). Additionally, there were unusual and lavish compensation deals with several vice-presidential appointments (disclosed during appointment confirmation hearings over the nomination of Jack Lew as Secretary of the Treasury). President Sexton and the Board of Trustees have since been busy apologizing and promising to do better in future consultation with faculty.

A significant experiment in shared governance involves Yale University and the National University of Singapore, partners in creating a new liberal arts college at NUS. Singapore, a wealthy city-state, has a repressive political system, raising questions about freedom of inquiry and expression at the new college. Those questions worried Yale faculty, but then President Richard C. Levin reduced the heat of an academic confrontation by heavily involving faculty in all aspects of creating the new college. Yale-NUS College emerged from a meeting of President Levin and President Tan Chorh Chuan of NUS at a World Economic Forum in Davos, Switzerland, in January 2009. Over the next two years, Yale administrators and senior faculty members travelled to Singapore and worked out a deal. The deal was announced March 2011. In April 2012, the Arts & Sciences faculty of Yale College passed a resolution expressing concern about Singapore's record on civil and political rights. But the resolution did not become a revolution. In May 2012, Pericles Lewis, a Yale professor of English and Comparative Literature, was named president of Yale-NUS College. Other top administrators were also named. In June 2012, faculty members were hired and began work on the curriculum. In December 2012, the American Association of University Professors (AAUP) made public a letter expressing concerns about academic and personal freedoms at Yale-NUS. The letter also asked Yale to make public all documents connected to the new College. Yale's public response was silence. Yale-NUS College's first class of 157 students arrived for orientation in July, 2013, and classes began in August.

The curriculum of Yale-NUS College is designed entirely by the faculty. Working in groups of 7 to 10, they wrestled with what to teach and how to teach it. Since there are no departments in the College, there was a high degree of interdisciplinary effort in the creation of the curriculum. The four-year program consists of 32 courses, 12 of which are part of a core. About one-third of the total course credits will comprise the major selected by the student. The issue of academic freedom was alive throughout. At one point, President Lewis told a *Wall Street Journal* reporter that, under the law in Singapore, students would not be permitted to hold political protests or form partisan political societies. Subsequently, he reversed himself and said that political debate *on campus* would be encouraged. To clarify matters, the faculty passed a resolution stating explicitly that free expression was a cornerstone of "our institution." Dean of the faculty Charles D. Bailyn stated that "fissile material" would be included in course content. Yale-NUS College reflects a high degree of administrator-faculty interaction and mutual respect. It will be fascinating to watch this experiment develop, with a presumably free liberal arts college functioning in a repressive governmental context.[1]

If a day comes when administrative authority establishes control over the diffuse but real power of the faculty, then the university's or college's ability to accomplish its missions will have been compromised. Well then, how likely is that unhappy outcome? It depends initially on faculty surrender of its power, not by a conscious decision, but by an erosion of its exercise. That depends, in turn, on the degree to which faculty attention focuses on research and external consulting, coupled with attractive compensation. All of which is time consuming, leaving little time for internal service devoted to the university's governance. Given this combination of trends, a power vacuum will be created. And administrative authority is not bashful about occupying the space. At some future time, if this trend continues, a tipping point could be reached, and administrative authority would effectively run the institution. At that point, academic freedom would be compromised, and in its death throes. We hope that such a point is never reached. In the end, it will depend on the faculty.

We come now to the several loci of real power in the university—board, president and administration, and faculty—and the need for consensus as a precursor of decisive action. Once again, we are at the deep end of the academic pool. Given the authority of administrative position and its potential conflict with the shared power of the faculty—often dormant but occasionally active—we are confronted by a significant impediment to consensus. Add to this the potential conflict of views over the nature of the academic mission between the faculty of the professional schools and the faculty of humanities in the Arts & Sciences, possibly buttressed by some law school professors, with a sprinkling of others from the professional schools. The former are prone to emphasize employability, with possible emphasis on obtaining a first job following graduation, while the latter are prone to favor a broad intellectual exposure that exercises the power of critical thinking, and prepares one for life. We face here the essence of the academic mission itself. Pragmatically, as well as philosophically, there must be room for both. To achieve a viable, if not happy and harmonious, consensus, there must be a marriage of different views. But that marriage may require a minister to arrange and officiate at the ceremony. In short, leadership is needed and that responsibility rests ultimately in the lap of the president. And he or she may have to exercise authority of position to achieve the goal; something especially likely in the face of a financial crisis, or a paradigm shift in perceptions of mission.

To gain a better understanding of faculty perceptions and likely reactions, one needs some insight into the psychodynamics underlying those perceptions and reactions. Such insight reveals a profound acceptance of the primacy of the doctoral degree in Academe—most particularly in research universities. That degree is the key to academic stature and advancement, perhaps most notably tenure. Possession of a doctoral degree has a further critical aspect; research (scholarly productivity) that results in the publication of books and articles published in learned journals. Research then becomes the second key to academic advancement and stature in those institutions. It becomes the primary criterion considered in achieving tenure, professorial advancement, and greater compensation. In short, it outweighs teaching and service to university governance as criteria for advancement. As a result, faculty attention to those criteria, especially service, is weakened, which explains their lessened willingness to participate in institutional governance, as well as the creeping advancement of administrative authority. It explains also the reduced teaching loads of research-strong faculty, and the concomitant impact on staffing profiles (a huge expansion in the use of contingent faculty and graduate teaching assistants). Finally, dissatisfaction among the latter groups fuels an interest in unionization, which poses further dangers to the research university's ability to accomplish its academic and employability missions.

Take note. What has just been said applies to research universities, not colleges and universities without doctoral programs. In the latter institutions, the major mission is teaching. Effectiveness in the transmission of knowledge, as well as the development of critical thinking, count most heavily. In terms of number of institutions and enrollments, they outweigh research universities. Of course research is not absent in the teaching institutions. However, it is directed there mainly to remaining current in one's field.

Budgets and fundraising have become oppressively dominant pressures consuming almost the entire agenda of the university or college president's daily calendar. That is the stated judgment of college and university leaders. It robs them of time for thoughtful consideration of institutional missions. Of course, money is a critical element enabling achievement of the missions, through staffing profiles that accommodate full-time, tenure-track professors in classrooms, as well as necessary plant and facilities. Unfortunately, their present controlling pressure on presidents imperils availability of time and thought directed at institutional missions. But the potential and ever-present danger is not robbing time alone. It extends to improper influence on academic matters—perhaps most frequently the admission of unqualified students—as well as the introduction of programs of study, or research Institutes or Centers that are not compatible with the institution's missions. The trick is to bring these pressures under control, so that academic and teaching primacy can be asserted. If that goal can be achieved—and we believe it can—then financial considerations will no longer overwhelm university and college presidents.

We come now to a consideration of conflicts of interest and Division I sports programs. Both are anathema to the integrity of the academic mission, being, as they are, threats to the core values of the mission. Conflicts of interest impact mission directly and significantly in both the classroom and the research lab. In the classroom, they contaminate integrity when a professor's pet ideas interfere with his or her objectivity, and prevent a fair and full presentation of all sides of an issue for student thought and consideration. This is also the case in the research lab. There it is the researcher's willingness to seek and accept evidence that undermines the criteria of transparency and consideration of contrary evidence. Also, willingness can be distorted by external consultation, richly rewarded, that influences the researcher's otherwise ardent desire to seek and discover truth. In both cases, the impact on research integrity is poisonous. We have suggested a solution that requires the establishment of a clearly stated policy, as well as the assiduous implementation of that policy by the university's or college's administration.

Division I sports programs are no less poisonous to academic integrity, corrupting, as they do, the primacy of academic affairs in institutional decisions. The distortion is discovered in the allocation of university or college resources, as well as in the coddling of misnamed *student/ athletes*. Both are serious problems. It is manifested also in the persistence of scandals involving sexual misbehavior by players and coaches; the most recent and most egregious examples being provided by the Sandusky case at Penn State. Perhaps the most damaging aspect of that case was the long-standing effort by the top administration of the university to cover up and conceal its occurrence, which enabled Sandusky to continue coaching and misbehaving. As a result, the university's reputation suffered severely as did its finances when a $60 million fine was levied by the NCAA. But, the Penn State case does not stand alone. The case of the University of North Carolina–Chapel Hill is equally damning. The creation of paper courses and course credits without any significant student/athlete performance, as well as the long-standing cover ups indict the university's administration. Not a year passes without other damaging illustrations where Division I programs compromise academic integrity. Misallocation of university resources is seen in the existence of university and college fees mandated for the support of athletic programs. It is evidenced also in institutional investment in professional-grade athletic facilities and stadiums.

What about the burgeoning number of non-academic administrators and employees in our universities and colleges? What have they got to do with institutional missions? Their existence has to be explained and justified, or they are an unnecessary and expensive growth on the academic body. In fact, they exist because they deal with real non-academic aspects of university and college life, i.e., the safety and comfort of faculty, students, and other personnel who carry forward the institution's missions. They are necessary, as they deal with a range of matters that impinge on the organization's daily life. We recall the terrible incidents of mentally ill people who killed and wounded innocent students and faculty whose security is vital. Transportation around the campus needs attention. In residential universities, important to the creation of a collegium and the fostering of intellectual interaction, transportation becomes a significant aspect of life. Buildings and labs require maintenance and service. Should these functions be performed in-house or outsourced? Unionization can become an issue. Faculty can and do resent the money required to perform these service functions as a drain, drawing resources away from the academic focus of the university. Neither resentment nor wishing will make them go away. They must be managed, and that is an inescapable reality.

C. Epilogue

Is the academic mission of our universities and colleges threatened? A flat, categorical NO! would be an incorrect answer. A flat, categorical YES! would be equally incorrect. Reality mandates an in-between world in shades of gray. In that real world, the question becomes: Are the threats of adherence to the ideals and values of academic integrity so compromised that they no longer rule, and it becomes generally accepted by society and academicians that indoctrination infects teaching, and manufactured evidence is treated as gospel? Above all, human inquisitiveness and probing curiosity are fettered and handcuffed by prevailing. fashionable ideas, most of which are intellectual garbage. In so terrible a world, freedom is gone, as is academic freedom and integrity.

Fortunately, we are able to conclude on an optimistic note. So long as society is free, academic integrity, though confronted by real threats—some of which are more serious than others—remains alive and viable. So long as society views the dangers as scandalous and unacceptable, academic integrity remains alive and viable. And so it is that our exploration of the question ends on an optimistic note.

Note

1. Karin Fischer, "Blurring Disciplines, Crossing Borders: Yale Helps Reimagine the Liberal Arts, with Asian Influences," *The Chronicle of Higher Education,* September 3, 2013, A24–A27.

Sources

Academe, March–April 2008, March–April 2009, March–April 2013.

Alfano, Michael C. "Follow-up to John Sexton's May 20, 2009, Memo Titled: *Re-engineering II.*" A memorandum to the NYU Community, June 1, 2009. NYU: New York, 2009. 1-9.

Bousquet, Mark. *How the University Works: Higher Education and the Low-Wage Nation*. New York: University Press, 2008.

Breneman, David W. and Chester E. Finn, Jr., eds. *Public Policy and Private Higher Education*. Washington, DC: The Brookings Institution, 1978.

Casement, W. "College Sports: Revising the Playbook." *Academic Questions*. Vol. 26, No. 1. Spring 2013.

The Chronicle of Higher Education. January 23, 2009, A 1, 12-14, 16, February 13, 2009, 16, February 27, 2009, A 1, March 27, 2009, A 1, A 22-23, April 24, 2009, A 1, A 16-18, May 1, 2009, A 16, April 17, 2009, A 11, September 4, 2009, A 27, September 4, 2009, A 26, February 12, 2010, A 80, February 26, 2010, A 25-26, March 26, 2010, A1, A 24, April 16, 2010, A 10, May 7, 2010, A 3, August 20, 2011, 20, August 20, 2011, 10, August 26, 2011, 28, August 26, 2011, 8, August 26, 2011, 23, August 26,2011, 22, August 26, 2011, 29, February 7, 2013, March 1, 2013, A 8, March 18, 2013, March 25, 2013, May 3, 2013, May 9, 2013, May 10, 2013, A 3, A 4, May 15, 2013, May 24, 2013, June 18, 2013, July 5, 2013, A 25, A 26, July 19, 2013 B 4, September 3, 2013, pp. A 24-27, October 8, 2013, November 8, 2013, A 2-4, November 11,

2013, Wired Campus, November 13, 2013, A 26, November 20, 2013, November 25, 2013, A 37, November 27, 2013.

Chronicle of Philanthropy. August 4–5, 2005, B, B1, B3.

Forbes. "The Business of College Football, College Football's Most Valuable Teams." January 19, 2012 and April 28, 2013.

Kerr, Clark, with Marian L. Gade and Maureen Kawaoka. *Higher Education Cannot Escape History.* Albany, NY: SUNY Press, 1994.

Hechinger, John. "SNHU, A Little College That's a Giant Online," *Bloomberg Business Week,* May 9, 2013.

Henderson, Rebecca, Adam B. Jaffe, and Manuel Trajtenberg. "Universities as a Source of Commercial Technology: A Detailed Analysis of University Patenting, 1965–1998." *Review of Economics and Statistics* 80, 1. Cambridge, MA. MIT Press. 1998. See http://www.mitpressjournals.org/doi/pdf/10.1162/003465398557221

Illinois Donors Forum Website. http://www.donorsforum.org/s_donorsforum/

Mehta, Jal, and Christopher Winship, *Moral Power.* Harvard University. See: http://scholar.harvard.edu/files/cwinship/files/moral_power-final_1.pdf.

Miami Herald. April 1, 2009, B1, April 26, 2009, 1A–2A.

NLRB v. Yeshiva University. 444 US 672–1980. No. 78–857. Argued October 10, 1979, and decided February 20, 1980.

The New York Times. April 2, 2009, B13, May 4, 2009, D1, 6, August 4, 2009, 14A, June 18, 2010, B14, June 22, 2013, A19, July 17, 2013, A1, A15, August 15, 2013, A20, August 25, 2013, 1, SP14P, August 26, 2013, A1, D4, November 13, 2013, A26, November 30, 2013, B11

Review of Economics and Statistics, 1998, 119–127.

Rosenzweig, Robert M. *The Political University: Policy, Politics, and Presidential Leadership in the American Research University*. Baltimore: Johns Hopkins University Press, 2001.

Wilson, Logan, *The Academic Man: A Study in the Sociology of a Profession*. New Brunswick, NJ: Transaction Publishers, 1942.

Shattock, Michael. *Managing Successful Universities*, SHRE and Open University Press. Berkshire, England. Second Edition 2010.

Statistical Abstract of the United States: 2012, US Department of Commerce, Washington, D.C., 2011, 178.

Taleb, Nassim N. *The Black Swan: The Impact of the Highly Improbable*. First Edition. New York: Random House, 2007.

University of Oregon. University Relations website: Public and Government Affairs. http://advancement.uoregon.edu/node/3

USA Today. April 28, 2013.

Zegers, Charlie."Highest Paid Coaches in Basketball," *About.Com:Basketball*, April 28, 2013. http://basketball.about.com/od/coaches/a/coach-salaries.htm

Index

and decision-making, 4–5
funding of (*see* Funding Sources;
  Fundraising)
and research faculty versus
  teaching faculty, 45–47
Reserves, retention of, 66–67
Revenue
and balancing expenditures, 73–
  75
Harvard Business Review as
  source of, 100
from licensing arrangements,
  102–103
Risk analysis, ethics and, 5
Royalties, for university-generated
  inventions and patents, 123–125
Rutgers University
Division I sports, programs at,
  159
Division I sports scandals at, 141–
  142

S
Safety, and service functions, 154–
  158
Salomon Brothers Center for the
  Study of Financial Institutions,
  and gifts inadequate for purposes, 92–93
San Jose State University, and
  MOOCs, 14, 16–17
SAT scores, and Division I sports
  programs, 135–136
Scandals
and Division I sports programs, 2,
  141–142, 187
in recruiting, 2, 141–142, 187
School of Business, New York
  University, high financial goals
  of, 94–96
Search committee, for university
  president. *See* President, search
  committee for

Selection, of university president.
  See President, selection of
Self-interest, 119
Service Employees International
  Union, universities as targets of,
  153–154
Service functions. *See also* Support
  services
in academic institutions, as a
  threat, 149–162
environment and safety, 154–158
examples of, 154–162
and human resources, nonacademic staff, 161–162
and information technology,
  hackers, 159–161
outsourcing of, 152–153
and sports facilities, 158–159
Shah, Niranjan S., and power of
  boards of trustees, 26–28
Short-term solvency, financial health
  and, 66
Snobbery, and doctoral degrees,
  48–49
Solicitations
for funds (*see* Fundraising guidelines)
for top leadership positions, 176
Solvency, short-term, 66
Sources, of funds. *See* Funding
  sources
Southern New Hampshire University, and online learning, 11
Spelman College, and faculty
  compensation survey, 61–62
Sports. *See* Athletes; Division I
  sports programs
Sports facilities, and service functions, 158–159
Staff
nonacademic, and service functions, 161–162

Truth, as goal of academic institutions, 2

U
Udacity
and MOOCs, 12–13, 14
and online graduate programs, 17–18
Unions and unionization
of academic staff, 45–62
of adjunct faculty, 58–59
authority and power and, 3
and Brown University case, 57–58
of contingent faculty, 57–62
of faculty, 54–57
and faculty power, 3, 57–58
of graduate teaching assistants, 57–62
and New York University case, 57–58
of outside contractors, 153–154
and Rensselaer Polytechnic University case, 56–57
universities as targets of, 153–154
Yeshiva University case of academic staff, 54–57
Universities and colleges. *See* Academic institutions
University employees, athletes as, 145–146
University Heights, and power of boards of trustees, 28–30
University image, and fundraising, 84
University of Alabama-Tuscaloosa, 113–116
and athletic program expenditures, 136–141
University of Arizona
and reductions in state aid, 73–74
and single source of funding, 68

University of Arkansas-Fayetteville, and athletic program expenditures, 136–141
University of California-Berkeley, and edX, 12–14
University of California-Irvine, and Coursera, 12–13
University of California-Los Angeles (UCLA), and corrupting influences of financial arrangements, 53
University of California system
licensing revenues of, 120
and single source of funding, 68
University of Chicago
Division I sports programs at, 133–141
graduate schools of, 50
and importance of teaching, 46
University of Florida, 113–116
and athletic program expenditures, 136–141
and faculty compensation survey, 61–62
licensing revenues of, 103
University of Georgia, and athletic program expenditures, 136–141
University of Illinois (Urbana-Champlain) case, and power of boards of trustees, 26–28
University of Kentucky
and athletic program expenditures, 136–141
coach compensation at, 169
University of Maryland, Business school of, 12
University of Miami, 113–116
Division I sports scandals at, 141–142
and students in support functions, 152

About the Authors

Abraham L. Gitlow is Dean Emeritus and Professor of Economics Emeritus of the Stern School of Business, New York University. The author of 15 books and numerous articles, he was a director of and consultant to a number of public corporations (Macmillan, Welbilt, Bank Leumi USA, etc.), as well as president of the East Ramapo School District Board of Education. An interdisciplinary thinker, his work embraced labor economics and industrial relations, management, and anthropology (his doctoral dissertation, The Economics of the Mt. Hagen Tribes, New Guinea, was published by the American Ethnological Society). Dr. Gitlow is a recipient of the University Medal of Luigi Bocconi University, Milan, Italy.

Howard S. Gitlow is Executive Director of the Institute for the Study of Quality, Director of the Master of Science degree in Management Science, and a Professor of Management Science, School of Business Administration, University of Miami. He received his PhD in Statistics (1974), M.B.A. (1972), and B.S. in Statistics (1969) from New York University. Dr. Gitlow is a Six Sigma Master Black Belt, a Fellow of the American Society for Quality, and a member of the American Statistical Association. He has authored or co-authored a dozen books.